LOVE
AND THE
WORLD

LOVE
AND THE
WORLD

A Guide to
Conscious
Soul Practice

ROBERT SARDELLO

LINDISFARNE BOOKS

Published by Lindisfarne Books
P.O. Box 799, Great Barrington, MA 01230

Library of Congress Cataloging-in-Publication Data

Sardello, Robert J., 1942-
    Love and the world : a guide to conscious soul practice /
Robert Sardello.
        p. cm.
    Rev. ed. of: Love and the soul. 1st ed. c1995.
    Includes bibliographical references.
    ISBN 0-9701097-4-1
    1. Conduct of life. 2. Spiritual life. 3. Soul.
    I. Sardello, Robert J., 1942- Love and the soul. II. Title.

BJ1581.2 .S24 2001
158--dc21   2001029208

Printed in the United States of America

9 8 7 6 5 4 3 2 1

For Karen, Marc, and Luke

And

Nicholas, Kathryn, Matthew, Samuel, and Christopher

CONTENTS

Acknowledgments

I THANK Paul Cash for an elegant job of editing this text. He brought clarity, warmth, a consistency of logic and the light of imagination out of what was otherwise a bumbling labyrinth of convoluted thoughts. Christopher Bamford, thanks for your continual support and for recognizing the importance of a spiritual psychology emerging from Anthroposophy. Michael Lipson took a great deal of care seeing this project through the steps from manuscript to the beautiful book you hold in your hand.

ROBERT SARDELLO

GETTING
STARTED

THIS BOOK presents a new psychology—a spiritual psychology. While new, it is based on the nearly forgotten definition of psychology as the science of the human soul. Soul in this sense is not something abstracted from our whole nature as beings of body, soul, and spirit. It is not abstracted from our engagement with others and with the surrounding world—nor from our relation with the spiritual worlds. My working definition of spiritual psychology therefore runs as follows:

> Spiritual psychology is an active practice that develops embodied, conscious, soul life to make that life open and receptive to the spiritual realms. This is done as an act of love toward ourselves, others, and the world.

This definition, I know, is very broad. Yet it took me eight years to come to these words, which summarize the content of this book.

Psychology, I want to claim, is more than the study of the human soul. One cannot conduct such a study without undergoing inner changes in the process. Psychology, since it is we who do it, necessarily implies that psyche studies psyche. It therefore belongs, by its very nature, to the realm of practice. It is not a theory wandering around seeking application. We must do our psychology rather than theorize about the soul. And, because soul is not abstracted from the world, the doing of psychology is the doing of love—consciously, actively, and for the sake of others and the world. It follows, too, that this is not only a book about psychology: it is also the very speech of psyche itself.

We live out our imagination of what constitutes being human. We think we know what human beings are: they are those people around us, apparently like us. Yet it may be difficult to put into words all we mean by this. The ancient and noble imagination of the human being as embodied soul and spirit, inseparably engaged with others, the world, and the spiritual cosmos, needs to be reformulated in the language of present-day experience. The languages of cosmology, alchemy, religion, and myth all convey something of the fullness of what it is to be human. They really amount to cultural memories that tell us how, in order to be human, we must enter into deep relationship with something larger and more significant than ourselves. And it must be larger, not only than our individual selves, but also larger than any familial, collective, religious, political, or social organization that claims to provide meaning.

We need now to find the ways to speak this degree of fullness in our own everyday language. This task constitutes a second aspect of the book. What is referred to here as the experience of the "I" expresses this spiritual aspect of the soul—the capacity to experience ourselves, others, the world, and the cosmos as spiritual activity rather than just as complex combinations of material substance.

The word capacity is a kind of key. It refers to a general ability. We have, for example, the capacity to speak; it is an ability characteristic of being human. The moment a capacity is actualized, it is no longer general, but specific and particular. We have the capacity to experience everything as spiritual activity. It takes a special alertness to the "I" to particularize this capacity into actual individual experiences. This book shows, in many different ways, how to go about realizing this capacity, which is equivalent to exercising the ability to love in creative ways.

The soul, like the spirit, is a deed we humans do. And it is a capacity—the capacity for life to be meaning, both felt and known. This capacity is realized when we have a conscious sense for images that flows through all modes of experience—from sensing to memory to dreaming to thinking. I define the soul very simply as myself. Myself, however, has nothing to do with the usual way we imagine ourselves, which is not soul but ego. Rather, soul as myself is the direct and immediate felt sense of uniqueness, not that I am, but that I am being given, and given at every moment. We can know our soul only through a primary act of self-love, which is not to love ourselves as if we were objects to ourselves, but rather, the dedicated work of being present to our depths.

We can dedicate ourselves to the depths which are the soul. This has been preserved as a tradition in psychology through the lively tradition of depth psychology with its emphasis on myth, symbol, dream, and image. Depth psychology, however, has always looked to the past in the defining of soul. Depth psychology sets the spontaneous image-making qualities of soul life (such as appear in dreams and imagination) in relation to symbol systems and myths from earlier cultures. We know we are in soul, says depth psychology, when we find ourselves living the collective unconscious.

This new psychology, however, shows a different relation of soul and time. The conjunction of soul and spirit in the human being is experienced as a felt current, coming toward us from the future. We know that we are in soul and open to the spiritual realms when, in a fully awake and conscious state, we live in the time of patient, not-knowing anticipation. This quality of not-knowing is a further act of primary love, and is akin to the experience of falling in love. When we fall in love, all is new, unknown, oriented toward what is to come, without knowing or needing to know what that might be. We step over the line of knowing based on past experiences, personal or collective, and enter into not-knowing, where for anything to make sense we now have to consciously feel the creativity of loving. Much of the world is in total confusion because we are being asked to develop this new capacity of living through conscious loving for the first time. Nothing makes sense anymore—relationships, economy, religion, civilization, education—the whole of the world now seems to be crumbling. And it is. But this is not the end. It is the beginning of having to develop entirely new capacities. I give numerous examples of how to go about doing this, and how to begin our development in a profound experience of love.

Besides re-imagining spirit and soul, this new psychology is fully embodied. The psychological tradition that has upheld the importance of soul, the depth psychology of C.G. Jung, also has the unfortunate distinction of being decidedly gnostic. I mean that a significant thread of Jung's psychology stems from that ancient religious tradition that views the body and the world as evil. The Gnostic religion holds the view that we are trapped in the body and in the world and the primary task is to find our way out and back to the fullness. Because the psychology of Jung and its further development have this gnostic streak, they typically have little to say about the body-as-soul. The view presented in this new psychology you are about to read is that the body is good and the world is good; more than that, the body and the world are sacred, holy, of soul and spirit substance. The chapter on sensing works to help us experience the body as not finished, but in the act of coming to be, every moment. The human body is being created in the acts of sensing. Sensing is the activity of the coming together of self with world, the meeting. Body is formed where world and self meet one another.

Jung's psychology cannot understand such a notion; consequently, there is no psychology of sensation in depth psychology. And Freud's psychology, while wonderfully affirming body, in its origins had a too mechanical notion of the body. A new imagining of the body is necessary if we are to find our way toward a fresh valuation of the world. The body, as described in this work, is an expression of love, and if we reach and search for spiritual love without realizing that love already permeates our organism, then we are practicing escapism rather than love.

This new psychology is also a world psychology. We have for too long now confined the notion of soul to the interior of the human being, leaving the world to the exploitation of need and greed. If there is no soul in the world, then the notion of the human being as having soul is nothing more than pious abstraction and bad theory. The notion of soul and spirit put forth in this writing weaves a fabric with the whole of the world. There is a very special myth expressing the World Soul, the stories told in all cultures of a spiritual being called Sophia. In all such stories, Sophia is not just another goddess. She is the world-as-imagination; she is the world-coming-to-be. She is God's light, and not "his" as his possession, but that through which God is able to see himself and to know himself and thus able to love all of creation, for God is love. That is what is at stake in this new psychology—as we work to experience this world in its intimate relation with the spiritual worlds.

All of the facets of this new psychology come together beautifully in the legendary tales of the Grail. I take the reader through just a small part of this story. The Grail stories, particularly Parzival, do not merely depict the world of chivalry and romanticism and wars. Rather, using the clothing of these twelfth-century images, they make a picture of the possible future of the human being. The Grail, while mysterious, is clearly not an outer object to be found somewhere. Each of us is already the Grail. We just have to realize it, and this process of realization is a task; it is our ongoing, daily work. It is our daily bread as well—a bread we share with others.

I am not the first to come up with this new psychology. All of the threads of it are to be found in the amazing work of Rudolf

Steiner and the anthroposophy that he founded. No one, however, has read Steiner with a psychological vision, and I must say, I feel this has been to the detriment of the valuable work of anthroposophy in the world. When anthroposophists express an interest in psychology, they have the usual notions of psychology in mind, hoping to update it to match the findings of Rudof Steiner. Psychology needs more than that; it needs to be totally re-visioned, top to bottom. We need to do more than try to apply anthroposophy to psychology. Anthroposophy provides the basis for re-imagining psychology altogether. This psychology can also work back and re-enliven the way anthroposophists work. This book presents a first effort in that direction.

A word about the goal of spiritual psychology. Can people be helped with spiritual psychology? Is there an alternative to the psychotherapies offered by current psychology? Yes, but helping will be quite new and different. It will be a therapeutic psychology of service. That is where the re-founding of psychology as a spiritual discipline of soul life in the world leads. What service is, however, will also have to be re-visioned. Taking the position presented in this book, it will be possible to come upon the other person as truly mysterious. It will be possible to meet the other person as the Good who brings out the good that is my own essence, knowable only in acts of service. And this act of serving, in turn, does not serve the other person as a separate self, but works toward the creation of love in the world.

I

TAKING THE SIDE
OF THE WORLD

THE FIELD of depth psychology, now about one hundred years old, is entering more and more into the public imagination. Who would have suspected a few years ago that books whose major concern is the life of the soul would be among *The New York Times* ten best sellers, two of them remaining there for nearly a year? The value of this interest in soul is enormous. People are feeling a deep urge to make soul work a central aspect of their everyday lives. They are not satisfied to leave this domain to professional psychotherapists. Most important, they will not tolerate living in a world devoid of the qualities of soul.

Soul-making as Research

Soul is a tremendously potent word, one that can act as a magnet for all sorts of interests that may relate only tangentially to how soul and its realm have been carefully cultivated by depth psychology through the years. For some, soul attracts religious concerns that have been ignored because of the connection with institutionalized religion and dogmatic authority. For others, it attracts lost values of imagination, story, myth, art, and aesthetics. And for others, it attracts the realm of mystery, concern for things that cannot be explained but are nonetheless felt as essential to life. For still others, it attracts the possibility of physical or emotional healing.

The pioneers of depth psychology were certainly aware of these factors, but they held one additional dimension to be of extreme importance—science.

Depth psychology is, among other things, centrally concerned with bringing together the ancient unity of religion, art, and science in ways suitable for modern circumstances. Healing has been taken to be a by-product of entering into this unity, but not its raison d'être. The originators and developers of depth psychology were first and foremost researchers into soul. They knew they had to be researchers because the nature of the phenomenon constantly spawns confusions that can be averted only by developing a constant vigilance of observation.

If I have anything to contribute to the widening of soul work as it gains some independence from professional practitioners, I hope that it is in fostering an interest in becoming researchers into soul in the broadest and deepest ways possible. Research has to be revisioned. It has to be taken out of the technological context of laboratory experimentation based on hypothesis, theory, and experimentation, and imagined more *as a way of life*.

Research also implies extending vision into areas not thought of before. Most significant of all, it not only involves uncovering and discovering what already exists; it also involves, in part, creating what is discovered. This aspect of research particularly characterizes the soul realm. Here we are not dealing with the inanimate world, or with the plant or animal worlds, where things can be approached as if they were fixed according to laws of nature (although in actual fact they are not). We are dealing with the distinctly human realm, where the creating factor is absolutely unavoidable. That is to say, the investigation of soul is also soul-making.

Research often begins with detecting the limitations of previous work in a given area. It does not usually have the aim of discrediting what has been done, but of extending insight into new areas, which often ends up requiring a revisioning of what has already been developed. As long as limitations go unnoticed, not only are new areas not opened up, but a part of the whole also continues to be viewed as if it were the whole.

The interest in taking depth psychology beyond the consulting room and into the world reveals two most interesting limitations of the field as practiced up until now. First, people have far more capacity to care for their own soul life than was envisioned by the founders of depth psychology, whose development of psychoanalysis concentrated on people who were unable to care for soul on their own. Second, and of more significance, depth psychology has not seen the necessity—now being enacted by those who wish to move soul-interest out into the world—of imagining that the world itself has soul. Further research, then, involves being able to observe the world carefully enough to see and understand the relation between the individual soul and the Soul of the World.

It is quite true that people now interested in soul work are not yet exactly clamoring to also experience soul in the outer world. Most feel more or less that soul work is primarily of personal benefit. This focus on personal benefits, I think, stems from taking the part of soul-research already developed as if it were the whole.

If the world did not have soul qualities that we increasingly feel as absent, we could be content to let psychology continue to concentrate only on people who cannot get on in the world. The people who are reading all these books and going to all these conferences, however, and taking up the schooling of their own soul, are decidedly healthy people. Are they not, in saying that the factor of soul is fast disappearing in the world, acknowledging that it must once have been there in some form?

The founding limitation of depth psychology can be pointed to as a deliberate and conscious turning away from the world. In two places, Sigmund Freud directly addresses the world as a problem for psychology. In *The Future of an Illusion* he states:

> For the principal task of civilization, its raison d'être, is to defend
> us against nature. . . . There are the elements, which seem to mock
> at all human control; the earth which quakes and is torn apart and
> buries all human life and its works; water, which deluges and drowns
> everything in a turmoil; storms, which blow everything before
> them; there are diseases, which we have only recently recognized as
> attacks by other organisms; and finally there is the painful riddle of
> death, against which no medicine has yet been found, nor probably
> will be. With these forces nature rises up against us, majestic, cruel,
> and inexorable; she brings to our mind once more our weakness and
> helplessness, which we thought to escape through the work of civ-
> ilization.[1]

Here psychology is not directly addressed, but we do have a
peculiar understanding of the role of civilization—and an equally
peculiar image of the natural world—put forth by the founder of
depth psychology. He describes the natural world, quite rightly, as
"she." He suggests that her qualities have to do with the elements—
earth, water, air, and, in place of fire, disease and death. And he
describes the elements only in their devastating aspects, not at all
in terms of their creating qualities.

Freud's view of civilization is of a defense against the soul qualities of the world. He finds this defense to be totally inadequate
and failed, and the work of psychoanalysis in building a strong ego-
sense is his way of buttressing up the capacity to keep the world at
bay. For Freud, a necessary detour in building a strong ego involves
turning to the soul realm. His way of turning away from the world
led to the modern discovery of soul life, but it is based in a completely different sense of the soul than that found in the ancient
tradition—where soul and world were never separated. (Heracli-
tus, for example, puts no limits on the soul, saying that one could
travel every road and never come to a place that is without soul.)

While in the statement above Freud seems to be opposing civilization to nature, and we might read psychoanalysis as a turn away

from nature, in another place it is clear that he is afraid of the whole world:

> Against the dreaded external world one can only defend oneself by some kind of turning away from it, if one is to solve the task by oneself. There is, indeed, another and better path: that of becoming a member of the human community and with the help of a technique guided by science, going over to the attack against nature and subjecting her to the human will. Then one is working with all for the good of all. But the most interesting methods of averting suffering are those that seek to influence our own organism. In the last analysis, all suffering is nothing else than sensation; it only exists in so far as we feel it, and we only feel it in consequence of certain ways in which our organism is regulated.[2]

Freud puts more faith in science than civilization as a good defense against the world. As we shall discover in chapters 4 and 5, however, while indeed science may be what has obscured the Soul of the World, it also, inadvertently, leads us to the possibility of rediscovering it. Even more significant, Freud here feels that psychoanalysis can be a way, not of alleviating human suffering, but rather of numbing the sensations of pain. If one cannot feel the onslaught of the "dreaded external world," then let it rip away; it does not matter.

But, it might be argued, depth psychology is of value precisely because it helps us to discover the most significant sources of pain. These lie in repressed traumas of early childhood, and through therapy we must, at least for a while, re-experience a great deal of pain that may have been expressed for years as unhealthy symptoms. The interesting suggestion provided above by Freud himself is that confronting all of that past pain may, just may, not have anything to do with resolving pain but only with numbing it.

If this turns out to be the case, the effects of such a procedure on the world would be quite devastating. If one becomes numb to soul pain, the suffering in the world would also not be felt. One might well look at suffering in the world and decry it, and even support efforts to do something about it; but one would no longer be able to feel someone else's suffering as if it were one's own.

We can imagine whole institutions and industries springing up for the purposes of alleviating suffering in the world. But if someone else's pain cannot be felt as if it were one's own, these institutions and industries would become part of the problem, because they would tend to perpetuate themselves as a helping industry. In the final chapter I look again at the importance of feeling, in healthy ways, the pain of the world and of others as if it were one's own.

The potential problems of the unseen limitations in the founding of depth psychology do not pertain only to psychoanalysis. Jung's psychology, for example, which I rely upon a great deal in this book, turns away from the world to the realm of archetypes or archetypal imagination. In this psychology, it is not we who suffer; our suffering is traced back to the pathologizing of the gods, and is not identified as only personal suffering. For Jung and his followers, what matters is not the world, but the eternal presences of gods and goddesses, now working through the soul and determining our behavior.

All forms of psychotherapy also suffer from this founding act of turning away from the world. People do not ordinarily talk in therapy about the ugliness of the environment, the devastation of the rain forests, rising crime, violence, homelessness, nuclear bombs, terrorism, joblessness, the terrible state of education, loss of beauty in the world, acid rain, the hole in the ozone layer, Bosnia, Somalia, or the Middle East—in short, they do not speak of the suffering of the Soul of the World. In therapy we talk about our dreams, relationships, fathers and mothers, depressions, anxieties, angers and hurts, archetypal figures, myths, and dysfunctional family systems. I cannot help but wonder in each case which part has been taken as the whole.

To question the limitations of depth psychology is not necessarily to question the whole enterprise. It may be only to question perpetuating the same form of the enterprise without researching new domains and larger dimensions.

Attention to soul in a conscious way is a truly new development in the world. For people who lived in times past, care of the soul was natural and instinctual. It was carried out through ritual, ceremony, mystery centers, oral traditions of story, myth, and art. But, while natural, it was not necessarily conscious in an individual way; it was most often a participation in an instinctual group or tribal consciousness. As consciousness has evolved in the direction of individuality, forms of care of the soul have needed to become more conscious and more individual.

We do not need a new theory. We need first to recognize the decline of the soul element in the world, and then to develop the kind of soul activity that can work against this decline. We also need to recognize how concern for the soul always carries the possibility of neglect of the world. This limitation of neglecting the world is not inevitable once a larger picture can be seen.

Researching the Ego

An additional limitation in the founding of depth psychology that makes it difficult to relate soul and world concerns the nature and function of the ego. Freud approaches ego quite differently than Jung does, but neither can get from soul to world via the ego. Here again Freud remains caught in his fear of the world. Regarding ego, he states:

> This little fragment of living substructure is suspended in the middle of an external world charged with the most powerful energies;

and it would be killed by the stimulation emanating from these if it were not provided with a protective shield against stimuli. . . . The protective shield is supplied with its own store of energy and must above all endeavor to preserve the special modes of transformation of energy operating in it against the effects threatened by the enormous energies at work in the external world—effects which tend toward a leveling out of them and hence toward destruction.[3]

The ego is for Freud our own little sense of ourselves, developed from past experience. In his view, it can be readily demolished by the dreaded external world and must develop defense mechanisms in order to constantly protect itself from being invaded by the world. These defense mechanisms need energy, and the source of this energy is the subconscious—providing it is not preoccupied with using energy to ward off the effects of past traumatic experiences. The ego thus does not take us into the world, but keeps us from it; it keeps us from it by compensating, idealizing, projecting, regressing, dissociating, sublimating, and some forty other kinds of defenses. Thus, in the face of the world, according to this view, the little sense of ourselves must continually struggle to maintain the experience of itself. We are always looking at the world through ego-colored glasses.

In Jungian depth psychology, ego is set in relation to soul and the question of world hardly enters at all. For Jung, ego is a result of the accumulation of personal experience, and he speaks of it as the center of consciousness. There is some concern among Jungians that the ego be strong—not because it may be overwhelmed by the world, but because it can be invaded by the contents of the unconscious, resulting in ego inflation. They do not concern themselves with the side of the world, but with the side of the soul. Analysts also concern themselves with ego taking itself to be the whole of consciousness, and thus also seek balance between ego and soul. (James Hillman, for example, understands ego to be that soul complex that takes itself literally.)

The limitation in this important aspect of depth psychology has to do with not recognizing the difference between ego and what is developed in the following chapter as the sense of the I. The I is not the same as ego. Ego is the result of the past, the accumulation of experience, the empirical sense of ourselves, which tends also to be identified with our body. The I is never fixed, has more to do with the future than with the past, is creative and free, and encompasses both individuality and world.

Because depth psychology does not recognize the I, it cannot effectively get from soul to world or from world to soul without taking them as two totally separate realms. The result is a tremendous narrowing of what psychology can be, because of the absence of a factor that binds individual soul with World Soul. This binding factor, as we shall explore, is the I.

Jung's psychology, in a certain sense, does recognize the I, there spoken of as the Self. But this Self is considered to result only from individuation of the soul, which comes from inner work, not world work. Because world is left out of consideration, the sense of the I as the Self moves with Jung in an Eastern spiritual direction, even though, paradoxically, he considers Christ as the archetype of the Self. The world, we are led to conclude, is *Maya*.

For depth psychology as thus far constituted, the way in which the ego has been conceived makes only one dimension of time important, the past. The conception of soul also relates only to the past, with both Freud and Jung. The I, however, as we shall explore it, is concerned more with the future than the past, more with what we can be than what we have been. While Jung's concerns have been rightly understood as teleological rather than as causes from the past that influence the present and future, his direction toward the future is from the past. I take teleology to mean *from* the future rather than *toward* the future. Research in this direction, I hope to show, is something quite new.

I must again emphasize that these important questions could

not even be raised if depth psychology had not been developed. Thus, I am trying to extend the boundaries of the discipline and give indications of a new orientation for research. The aim is not to suggest that depth psychology is wrong, only that it is not something to be taken and used as a technique because it is not finished.

Further, the very nature of the enterprise is to remain unfinished. To become involved in the work of the soul, I am suggesting, is to become a researcher, something that is asked of and available to anyone. This form of research is not to be left to the professionals alone, who too easily become engaged in defending territories. This research initiative does not involve a special laboratory, equipment, funding, and publishable results. It belongs to everyone. All that is needed is a sense of soul, presence to the immediacy of the world, and care.

Soul and Body

What I keep looking for in depth psychology is concern for the world. Thus, this first part is an exploration of the space of my discipline, looking for a door or a window into the outside world. Perhaps this opening can be found in the way the body is approached in depth psychology. After all, in everyday life our body locates us in the world. Let us again begin with the founder. How does Freud imagine the relation between soul and body? In one way, for Freud, soul is the same as body. However, he holds to a most mechanistic conception of body, leading him to speak of psyche or soul as an apparatus. For example, in *The Interpretation of Dreams*, he speaks in this way of psyche and body.

> All our psychical activity starts from stimuli (whether internal or external) and ends in innervation. Accordingly we shall describe a sensory and a motor end to the apparatus. At the sensory end there lies a system which receives perceptions; at the motor end there lies

another, which opens the gateway to motor activity. Psychical process advances in general from the perceptual end to the motor end. This however does no more than fulfill a requirement with which we have long been familiar, namely that the psychical apparatus must be constructed like a reflex apparatus. Reflex processes remain the model of every psychical function.[4]

This quite paradoxical statement leads to an inescapable conclusion: that for Freud body has no soul, and in fact, for Freud, soul has no soul. Does that mean that everything is world? Hardly. I am sorry to say that it means that all is mechanism, mechanics; we are automatons, and *body* and *soul* are only two words that stand in for reflex processes. Freud is a wonderful depth psychologist when he functions as a therapist and observer; but the moment he starts to think about his observations, he is utterly bound to nineteenth-century mechanistic science.

Because the sense of the body is everywhere dominated by biology and medicine, even in psychology, we have to look more at the ways that some depth psychologists work in practice to relate soul and body than at what they say about the relationship. While there is no question that there is a connection, body itself generally is understood as more or less a middle ground, belonging neither to world nor to soul.

An analytic psychologist, for example, may relate ulcers and the processes of soul. A typical interpretation states that a gastric ulcer is an expression of an unconscious desire to be fed, a longing to be pampered and cared for in an unconscious regression to the oral phase of development. The stomach reacts to the unconscious wish to be fed by acting as if the stomach itself is food to digest and thus begins to digest itself, which leads to an ulcer.

This kind of interpretation most likely tells us more about the rich fantasy life of the interpreter than it does about the person suffering from ulcers. While the interpretation does in fact assume that body is soul, the basis for such an assumption needs to be examined and described. The interpretation also strings together a host of unfounded assumptions—that of unconscious wishes, regression, an oral developmental stage that lingers on in the unconscious, all of which are somehow working in or on the body.

How dreams may symbolize body processes is also attracting widespread interest. For example, in Marc I. Barasch's *The Healing Path: A Soul Approach to Illness*, Jungian psychologist Meredith Sabini is quoted as saying that the state of the body is symbolized in dreams by the condition of an object like a house or a car.[5] A car's headlights are like the eyes, the four tires are like the body's limbs, the electrical system is like the nervous system, and hoses have to do with circulation. Unfortunately, we here also have an extraordinarily reductionist sense of the body, reflecting more this psychologist's lack of understanding of the body than anything else.

The interweaving of soul with body, which will be discussed in chapters 7 and 8, opens up in quite a different way once we have a view of the Soul of the World. The limitation of depth psychology in this area stems from conceiving the body as an entity rather than an activity, a material substance rather than a metamorphosis of soul into substance.

Apocalypse Now

Returning to the observation at the beginning of this chapter: What could possibly be going on in the world that brings about the desire to pursue questions of the soul at this time? At first, I suspected that fear played a large role. Few living in present times do not feel that everything is breaking down. In addition, a change of millennium always brings with it great fears of the "final" end. Are people turning to care of the soul as a final preparation? Fear, I suspect, is part of the answer, but only the most superficial part.

This new millennium, I suspect, brings not the end of the world, but the beginning of the feminine world. Soul, in all places and in all times, has been felt to be feminine. A significant aspect of the present interest in soul is that it coordinates and works in tandem with interest in the goddess. This book has as a central concern Sophia, Wisdom, Soul of the World. Rudolf Steiner, who has been the inspiration for this book, said in 1911 about the coming millennium:

> We must eradicate from our souls all fear and terror of what comes toward us out of the future. . . . We must look forward with absolute equanimity to all that may come and we must think only that whatever comes is given to us by a world direction that is full of wisdom.[6]

The word *wisdom*, here, refers to Wisdom, Sophia, the Sophia of the Apocalypse:

> A great and wondrous sign appeared in heaven: a woman clothed with the sun, with the moon under her feet and a crown of twelve stars on her head. She was pregnant and cried out in pain as she was about to give birth. (Rev. 12: 1-2)

Fear is indeed present, but so also the approach of the Sophia. Sophia is more than a goddess figure, an archetype, an imaginal presence, the feminine conceived as having to do with women. Chapter 3 develops something of what she is all about and her world significance, indeed, her significance as world. I feel strongly that the emerging urgency of feeling toward soul is a preparation for a Sophianic world. This preparation has happened twice before, with tragic results.

Trevor Ravenscroft and T. Wallace-Murphy, in *The Mark of the Beast*, trace the history of the number 666 in world history, based on the research of Rudolf Steiner.[7] The year 666 A.D., they say, marked the founding of the Academy of Jundi-Shapur in Persia. This academy came about as a result of the closing down of the famous Greek academies, most notably the Greek schools of philosophy, which were terminated by Emperor Justinian, who wished to sweep away all pre-Christian knowledge. The exiled Greek philosophers journeyed to Persia and set up a new academy. Over a number of years, the direction of the work of this academy was altered from a concern that we could now speak of as a concern for soul and world to a concern for the first foundations of the development of materialistic science. It was here, for example, that medicine, which prior to this time still understood the body as soul substance, began to be transformed into a more technical medicine of the human organism. It was here also that knowledge of the physical world changed from a sense of the Soul of the World to materialistic physics. This first emergence of the Sophia was thwarted, giving us science instead of a unity of science, art, and religion.

Twice 666 is 1332. In that year, Philip the Fair brought about the downfall of the Knights Templar, an order devoted to the Sophia. The work of the Knights Templar was extraordinary, and is dealt with more extensively in chapter 9. They invented the system of credit and made enormous amounts of money by holding monies for wealthy travelers so that they would not risk losing it to bandits while on pilgrimage. When the travelers reached their destination, they could withdraw funds at their place of arrival. It was the beginning of the modern banking system.

What was most extraordinary about the Knights Templar is that they never used their profits for themselves. They instead used the funds to make things in the world of a soul nature—cathedrals, hospitals, charities, public art. The idea was to bring soul to expression in the world of built things—things as image.

Philip the Fair wanted the money possessed by the Knights Templar and thus accused them of heresy. The Knights were tortured, made to admit things that they did not do, and killed. Again, Sophia did not come into expression as soul in the world. Instead, this takeover by Philip was the beginning of economics as making profit instead of making soul in the world, and now we have a world dominated by concern for money as profit.

Thrice 666 is 1998. Might this date mark once again the possible development of a Sophianic world as well as a crisis in its unfolding? What we have had as depth psychology can be seen in such a context as no more than a preparation—developing an outlook and the capacities needed to shift world views, sensitizing the imagination, awakening the potential unity of science, art, and religion, and, most important, focusing on the individual rather than on a system.

As for bringing these capacities into the wider world, this movement has not yet even begun. The danger lies in taking the preparation as the outcome. The form that this danger could easily take is that of using soul for our own purposes rather than for the sake of the world. If this happens, then fear of the world would increase, resulting in taking apocalypse literally. If soul, image, depth, mystery, myth, dream, interiority, quality, beauty, unity, wholeness apply only to the individual soul and not to the world, then as far as the outer world is concerned we are all fundamentalists. As long as soul development proceeds only with regard to people and not with regard to the world, then it is precisely this development that is at the same time producing fear of apocalypse. The contrast between what one experiences in an inner way and what one finds in the world becomes more severe and more split off from inner life.

If the first possibility of a Sophianic world resulted in the foundations of materialistic science instead of the development of the knowing through soul, and the second possibility resulted in economics for self-interests rather than for building a world of soul, what might result if the third possibility does not bear fruit? Let us imagine all those who work in the realms of soul as if they were members of an academy such as the Academy of Jundi-Shapur, or members of a group of world-soul makers such as the Knights Templar. This academy or this group is no longer an enterprise located in a specific place; the members are scattered and their ties are invisible, but nonetheless real.

Feeling such invisible bonds may be the most important work to be done in the present. All of those soul books that are now reaching a larger world may be imagined as a call put out into the world to begin to locate who belongs to this invisible community. Such a call also would indicate that a crisis is at hand, that once again it is entirely possible that Sophia will be denied.

The denial this time will result in the making of a new world, just as the two previous denials resulted in materialistic science without soul and economics without imagination. This time the new world will be virtual reality, extending far beyond what is currently possible. Virtual reality is an imitation of soul in the world. As explored in a later chapter, virtual reality imitates fantasy, dream, creativity, interiority, but it is a turn against the world. Virtual reality in fact makes the world seem totally unimportant, is addictive to itself by turning soul into entertainment, and leaves the outer world totally exposed to exploitation.

The possible unity of science, art, and religion, which is central to the impulse of depth psychology, is also at risk. The first aspect of this unity was damaged when science turned away from the Soul of the World. Now, however, we see signs of science and medicine becoming again concerned with soul. The second aspect of this unity was damaged when the art of making things in the world that express soul turned instead to making money. There are many signs that a world dominated by economic concerns is now breaking down. New senses of economy as care for the world could emerge. The third aspect of this unity would be damaged by taking the inner world of the individual to be the only temple of soul. Whether we can take up the task of a true imagination of the world hinges on whether it will be possible to take depth psychology's preparation and begin the work of taking the side of the world.

2

INDIVIDUALITY
AS LOVE

THE ANCIENT MAXIM "Know Thyself" has come to mean "Turn inward and away from the world." Self-knowledge, however, actually means knowing, experiencing, feeling, sensing, the world fully. We know ourselves through the world, and the world is enhanced with our every act of self-knowledge. The emphasis throughout this book is on working on a new soul practice—one aimed at expanding our experience of the ego to the point that the sense of who we are incorporates all of the world, which at the same time means that where we find our individual soul is in all of the world. My intent is to promote a fully healthy ego to which nothing is foreign, nothing is excluded.

Goethe expressed a similar goal for humanity: "When a man's healthy nature works as a whole, when he feels himself to be living in the world as in a great and beautiful and worthy whole, when this harmony brings him a pure, free joy, then the universe, if it could come to be aware of its own self, would cry out in exultation at having reached its goal and would marvel at the height which its own being and becoming had attained." Here we find a spiritual ideal that is not founded on self-renunciation, turning away from the world, or working to rid oneself of ego. In fact, to live up to Goethe requires healthy ego development. Here, ego development may be confused with egotism, but they are not the same. The difference, however, needs careful attention.

Egotism means that one is self-centered, self-absorbed. We usually picture an egotist as someone who has little self-awareness and holds tightly to that small awareness, afraid that it could be taken away. Here, the ego wants to be unique, different, special; it becomes jealous when others seem to be the focus of attention and defends itself through competitiveness and authoritarianism. This ego is actually weak and seeks isolation; it mistrusts others and the world. Such a person is not truly an egotist at all, but a fearful person who has been deeply hurt and wounded. Another example is someone who is interested in matters of the world, matters of soul, matters of spirit—someone who has pursued development. Such a person might appear to be quite noble, but if these interests have been pursued primarily as a mode of self-development, what we have is still an egotist—a noble egotist.

The range of self-centeredness can and often does extend into an egotism of soul and of spirit. Soul work is inevitably egotism when the sole intention of such work is to find out more about oneself, or to form a better connection with the soul realm, or even to live by the guidance given from the soul realm, unless at the same time we seek to know the outer world more fully through such work. Likewise, spiritual work is inevitably egotism when it means to "know thyself" as if one were separate from the world, or to "look for God within" as if there were nothing of a spiritual nature to learn from the world or about the world.

Expanded forms of egotism are no less egotistical than ordinary self-centeredness. In fact, these forms are more dangerous because they make us feel as if we have entered into something larger than self-centeredness—the soul or the spirit—while in fact we have simply changed the vocabulary of self-centeredness from "what I want" to "what my soul wants" and "what my spirit wants," which removes us even further from the world. Soul work and spiritual practice are often entered into for our own advantage. The possibility of inner work going in this direction is heightened to a high degree in the present world because there is so much fear in the world that one tends to seek inner development as a defense against the world. Inner development can be a way of getting through what seems to be a cruel, harsh, and violent world, a way of saying, "This world cannot hurt me."

The difference between egotism and a healthy, fully awake I-consciousness can be expressed as the difference between individualism and individuality. Individualism consists of a one-sided development of the ego. Here, the ego may take in all the surrounding world has to offer, all the soul realm has to offer, all the spirit realm has to offer, but it does not create anything from what has been received. Individuality, on the other hand, consists of continually giving out to the world as a response to the act of taking in what the world offers. The word *create* expresses the particular quality of meeting the world through individuality, a quality that goes beyond individualism because what is returned to the world is something truly new. But the act of creating is capable of being captured by the more self-centered world of individualism, where it becomes a self-conscious aim to be different and unusual. Thus, we must look deeply into this act, which implies that individuality is spontaneous and conscious but not self-aggrandizing.

"The rose adorns herself in order to adorn the garden," says Rudolf Steiner. So individuality is not for oneself, but for the world. How can this come about? When the rose is as beautiful as it can be, it adorns the garden. Further, the beautiful rose cares not whether anyone is around to behold its beauty. The rose draws all that it needs from the surrounding and gives out beauty in return. The plant takes in substances from the earth, the light, the rain, the influences of the moon and the seasons, the care of the hands that tend it, and gradually transforms all of this and more into the flower. Beauty is not an accidental quality of the rose, but the rose being a rose, doing what a rose does.

Individuality acts in a similar manner. That is, individuality is not something one has or even something one is. Individuality is an act—the act of inner, conscious awareness shaping, forming, and interiorizing the essence of each moment of experience, endowing experience with reverence and love, thereby individualizing what presents itself to consciousness. We could say that individuality is a concentration of the whole world at the site of every person— potentially. What exists in the outer world as spread out in space and time, lives as the inner life of soul and spirit. We are called to make ourselves in the image of the world, excluding nothing, taking it all in and transforming it through love. Individuality, because it concerns not just being open to the world, but also transforming through love what is experienced, may be the highest calling of a loving devotion to Sophia, the Soul of the World. How can this come about? How can individuality be developed?

Developing Individuality

The beauty of the rose occurs naturally, but we must create our own individuality. Error and confusion constantly creep in to cloud this act. On one hand, organized religion says that a divine world order is the creation of the gods and that the task of human beings is to submit to this order. On the other hand, depth psychology takes the same view but places it in the realm of the soul, saying that the inner life is also governed by the gods and that the task of human beings is to submit to the gods within. Those who take up the practice of soul work gradually come to be able to determine "want the soul wants" and how that may differ from the way one is actually living.

The difference between religion of an outer order and the religious nature of soul work as practiced by depth psychology is that the former establishes outer laws and practices to be followed uniformly by those who take up that religion, while the latter establishes what pleases or displeases the gods on a more individual basis. In the first instance we have a group religion while in the second we have an individual religion.

What I wish to make clear is that individual religion is not the same as individuality. Religion, either outer or inner, asserts that its wisdom stems from God or the gods. Individuality recognizes no such guidance; rather, it takes responsibility for experiencing everything of the world as manifestations of soul and spirit realities and for establishing free intercourse with the world as endowed with soul and spirit.

To begin creating our individuality, we must be more radical than organized religion and more radical than depth psychology. We must be able to sense the power of an act of creating that is solely and completely human, and, further, we must take full responsibility for this act. Only then will we be able to traverse soul and spirit realms, and meet what we find as friends and co-workers rather than as higher powers to which we must submit ourselves. Eastern practices avoid this responsibility by seeking to dissolve the ego, while Western religions avoid it by submitting the ego to higher powers.

Depth psychology avoids this responsibility by internalizing both Eastern and Western views—the ego submits to the gods within, and then gradually gives way to the Self. By not confronting the human power of creating oneself, we also ignore the responsibilities involved in this act. Thus, more and more, human creating takes all sorts of perverse forms as the human "I" is concealed as the true creator. Weapons of incomprehensible destructiveness are created anonymously, shifting responsibility from the creating act to ethical questions concerning how and when such weapons should be used; Ionesco and Beckett celebrate the disappearance of the I from human reality; biologists clone genes, leaving to others the problems of what to do with such creations. In all such creating, we are creating ourselves, without taking responsibility for the act, both during and following the act.

There is something undeniably frightening and threatening about speaking of the I, about trying to describe its activity. We can hardly conceive of allowing such a reality to exist, for the implications would seem to include loosing onto the world freedom from outer regulation, law, society, religion, morality, even community. Can people be allowed to be themselves? Is not individuality the same as anarchy? If such an image comes to mind it is because we imagine that desires, passions, the darker and more hidden aspects of the soul would be released if all outer forms of civilizing influences were no longer in effect. More accurately, we imagine what would happen if one who is more or less ruled by such forces were suddenly to be free of outer restraint of any sort. In such cases, passions, instincts, and desires would define who one is, so a healthy ego consciousness is the only hope. Most importantly, individuality is not something that just appears if everything else is removed; it must be the object and aim of development.

Individuality does not come naturally; it cannot be given to anyone, and it cannot be taken forcibly by anyone. It is a path of development, the path of love.

There are, it seems to me, three aspects to this development: first, the development toward the experience of the I; second, the development of feeling; and third, the development of purpose. These three spheres constitute the components of individuality. They do not exist side by side, and they do not develop one before the other in sequence. These three components are not isolated within us, but are at the same time within us and within the world. Thus, their development is contingent upon attentiveness to the world.

The Experience of the I

The human "I" is everywhere deprived of its reality. Even when it has asserted itself in human history, as it did with the blossoming of the natural sciences in the sixteenth century, the true capacities of the I have remained hidden. While the natural sciences did go so far as to "clear" the inner and outer world of the projected presences of divine beings to be submitted to, thus opening the possibility of understanding the laws of natural processes, they stopped short. Natural scientists remain unaware that the laws they discover are at the same time creations of their own spirit-activities in conceiving these laws and their own soul-activities of imagination.

Galileo, for example, saw a church lamp swinging and was led to find the laws by which a body swings. He did not see that the laws that made his experience comprehensible were of his creation. He did not simply discover some natural process, but in fact added to the world an act of his own true individuality. I am not saying that Galileo impressed his subjectivity onto the world; rather the breakthrough was an act of his individuality uniting with the world. The point of individuality is that by creating, it creates what is actually there—albeit not there in the form of comprehension, but only in the form of perception, until the creative act of comprehension takes place. Then the world rejoices, for it has become more whole; perception and comprehension together reveal the world more fully. The mistake of the natural sciences is that, until very recently, scientists believed they simply discovered the laws of the natural world, not recognizing that their observations were also creating in part what was being observed.

We can begin now to approach the true mystery and grandeur of the human I. What is most immediately striking, if we approach the sense of the I without bias and completely fresh, is that nothing accounts for the existence of the I. The experience "I am an I" appears quite spontaneously. No one is instructed or has to be instructed from outside about its existence, nor does it appear from inside as a gradual accumulation of experience. We are not born with this capacity to say "I"; it appears quite spontaneously, at about the age of three. What we feel about our sense of ourselves can be influenced from the outside, but its existence is not given by anything other than itself. The I posits itself and is also the result of that positing. The I is at one and the same time subject and object, activity and the content of that activity. Egotism occurs through paying attention only to the content and not to the activity by which the I is continually creating itself as a content.

This description of the I does not result in subjectivity, in positing an I that is inside us and over against the world outside. That individuality is at the same time a world phenomenon can be seen in the following description by Walter J. Stein who remembered his first experience of being an I:

> In my earliest memory-picture I see myself standing in the middle of a road on a wooded height, a little insecure on my little legs, faced with the task of crossing the road alone and unaided. The woman who is looking after me has hidden behind the trunk of a tree, and I know for certain that she is there and she is not my mother. The lady is obviously making an experiment to see how independent the little man has become. . . .
>
> Simple as the incident is, it is of great importance in the totality of my life, for at this moment I first became aware of the fact that I was an I. The feeling of having to direct my little body alone and unaided across the road gave me this experience in consciousness. I did not feel my self in my little body at all, but spread out all around it, and where I felt my self to be was not only not in the body, it was not even near it. . . . I had the distinct experience of being spread out over the whole surrounding scene. My self included the whole width of the road and, too, the neighboring trees, including the one behind which my governess was hiding. I still remember the inner feeling of delight it gave me to know that she imagined she was hidden from me, while actually my self was spread out over the space in which she was. She and the tree were within my experience of self, and though the little body down there felt something like fear at being left alone, the true self rejoiced in this fear and in the feeling, "I am an I" which went with it.[1]

This small memory holds great wisdom, and provides insight into the full experience of the I as creator and content, in oneself and in the world. This memory cannot be called an "out of body experience," a projection of the self into space, for there is the dual awareness of "being here and there" at the same time. We do not recognize this kind of experience all of the time because the warmth of the body is different from that of surrounding things, giving the impression of the self attached to the body but not the world. Being a body also means that the I, unless effort is asserted to regain its presence as also belonging to the world, can and does come to be identified with the presence of the body. The I is easily put into servitude, becoming limited to what the body needs for its survival and comfort. This is I reduced to personal ego.

While in the above memory experience the I is felt to be spread over the immediate surroundings, it is by no means limited by geographical boundaries. The I extends to the highest star. Ancient wisdom understood this fact. Plutarch, for example, says: "In addition to the part of the soul which is submerged in the earthly body, the human being has another and purer part, hovering outside him like a star above his head. This is rightly called his Daimon or Genius." But as soon as we start to get cosmic like this, we can feel the pull to bring in religious and esoteric concepts and start talking about the gods.

If we refrain for a moment, we can describe a further aspect of individuality. Being one with our Daimon or Genius, each of us is responsible for our own destiny. Our Genius, or guide, is beyond us, but not detached from or other than us. This assures that our destiny is the same as our individuality. Destiny is not something under the control of the gods, not something that comes to us out of the cosmos, because we belong as much to the cosmos as we do to the earth. That is to say, our life is dependent upon nothing outside, but is the creation of the I. The I that understands itself can make itself dependent upon nothing other than itself, and is answerable to nothing other than itself. And, it is important to emphasize that the I spoken of here is the incarnate, embodied I, not any general and abstracted notion of the I.

The I as described here is not available as an experience of ordinary consciousness. In truth, we are nearly all, at the very best, noble egotists. Few individuals have achieved individuality. What would be required? Everything of a general nature that we might say about ourselves must be thrown off. I am more than a man, more than a woman, more than a Jew or a Christian or a Muslim. I am more than one who thinks, for the next moment I can change my mind and destroy what I just thought. Further, ideas are something general; I am not an idea. We must experience our own I; it is not an idea. Any idea is too poor to encompass that which can bring ideas out of itself. There is nothing fixed about the I. I cannot be defined by race, religion, community, society; if I participate in any of these structures, it is a completely free association. I am not what I do insofar as this is in any way regulated from without; I am not my past or the accumulations from it. I am an I.[2]

To experience individuality requires being able to stay always within the process. In relation to the world, this means that the world, which is also encompassed within the I without thereby being simply my subjective experience of the world, is not fixed but is also constantly mobile. The world is an object for me only insofar as my experience of myself becomes objectified, which means that my I has been identified with the place of my body. This state of identifying ourselves with our physical body is the result of a long historical objectification of the world.

Feeling

Passions, instincts, desires, and emotions are not denied or avoided in coming to the experience of individuality, but are fully felt and entered into as consciously as possible. We are governed by our passions, instincts, desires, and emotions whenever we become detached from experiencing the wider world. Because we are not attentive to the world, the feeling that is present in every aspect of the world—the beauty of the world, given through the particularity of each thing of the world being exactly what it is—goes unnoticed. The beauty of the world is nonetheless a powerful force.

Beauty in the world is experienced by the individual as feeling. Feeling is more than a response to beauty; beauty is not the cause of feeling, but feeling is the consciousness of beauty and therefore belongs as much to the world as it does to us. Feeling can be the educator of passion, instinct, desire, and emotion, bringing them out of the dark where they are experienced as chaotic into full relation with the world. Since we are ordinarily not in very good connection with the world, passion, instinct, desire, and emotion serve as poor substitutes for feeling.

If we look more closely at beauty and try to describe more carefully the beauty of the world, we do not arrive at aesthetics, but rather love. Is not beauty the particular way in which the world expresses itself as love? We can tell that this is indeed so by attending to the feeling present in the moment of perceiving something beautiful. At that moment what we feel is love, the interior presence of beauty.

What we usually call feelings are no more than abstractions, because they lack the particularity that can come only through a united presence with the individual things of the world. Without the presence of the world, feelings are more or less unformed complexes of passion, desire, and emotion. The capacity to feel the presence of beauty depends upon the awareness of the I. Feeling is not essentially different from the I, but is a particular mode of operation of the I, the individual presence to the world not as an array of objects and things, but as rhythm, movement, tension, musicality, drama, mobility—the world as verb and adjective rather than noun, as activity rather than entity.

If several artists stand before the same landscape and then paint this landscape, several entirely different pictures will result. Each artist will paint exactly what he or she sees, but what is seen depends upon individuality. One might see the activity of the atmosphere of the landscape; another, the form and line; another, the contrasts among hills, sky, water, trees, rocks. Even if two of the artists focus on the same activity, their paintings will nonetheless be decidedly different; such is the individuality of the world in its display of itself as beauty.

The artists, in order to express what is actually there, must approach what is there out of their own complete individuality. But to paint what the landscape made them feel, they must attend to its beauty, experience what the landscape feels like, not their subjective responses to it. They have to paint what they see in its immediacy of presentation, which includes their immediacy of feeling, thereby revealing the reality of the landscape now individualized.

When we see the world as an array of objects, things, and events, we are seeing conceptions of the world rather than the world in its beauty. This sort of seeing is egotistical rather than individual because we are relying on fixed notions, and even fixed feelings, about the reality in front of us rather than engaging with the immediacy of the world. In this way of approaching the world, nothing can be learned from the world; no wonder, no surprise, no insight can be gained into oneself. When we approach the world with such an absence of feeling, boredom and psychological unease enter because passion, desire, and emotion have no way to individualize.

One might certainly think that this way of considering feeling in relation to the I might be beneficial in understanding the natural world. But in the constructed world of modern civilization, to approach life with the kind of openness I am suggesting seems impossible. We are faced with so much technology, media, information, entertainment, violence, and propaganda in everyday life that it seems necessary to develop a numbness, an an-aesthesia to what is around us. The world of daily life hardly seems to be the place of beauty through which individuality might come into creation. The world of nature does not even exist any longer, for the interrelationships of nature have been interfered with to the point that we now have no more than fragments of nature. In speaking now about the world as the location of beauty, and as the source of love and feeling, are we engaged in a romantic fantasy having to do with something that no longer exists?

The answer to this dilemma once again is approached through our inquiry into the nature of the I. With the ordinary sense of ego-consciousness, confronting the present world and being truly open to what appears would drive one into immediate madness. The senses would be overstimulated; we could not meet what presents itself, and would have a very diminished sense of who we are as human beings. To meet the world, the I needs to be strengthened, and this only comes about through effort.

This effort begins with striving to be open to the world, even if for only a few moments each day. But the practice must be regular. Gradually, changes will result. One might well want, for example, to try to enter the feeling world through the back door, through paying attention to dreams rather than to the world. Or, one might try to enter through giving attention to the arts—to painting, music, dance, ritual, drama, poetry. But, in our time, the hardening forces of the constructed world meet us everywhere and are much stronger than the feeling life that could be cultivated through these means. Delving into the imaginative world of the arts or into dream life excites possibilities that cannot be sustained when one returns to ordinary life. On the other hand, if one takes up the development of the I, then art and dream can follow along without the accompanying sense that one must find some way out of the harshness of the world in order to live in connection with soul and spirit realms.

Though the I is not bound by the fragmented world, it does not flee the world's apparent lack of beauty and imaginative qualities. Even while the natural world is so fragmented that the interrelationships of everything to everything else in nature are not immediately apparent, the fragments still show traces of this quality when one learns to observe. A patch of greenery in the middle of a large city, for example, develops its own ecosystem.

Ecology and the efforts to care for endangered species have to do with a dim sense that if these interrelationships are completely destroyed, human physical survival is not the only thing at stake, because long before that disaster the human soul and spirit would become unable to function. We feel this in brief moments in which we are awake to what surrounds us; what is most striking at first is not the ugliness of the constructed world, but the banality of sameness that characterizes much of what we have made of the world.

How is it that the I is capable of recognizing that this is not what the world is meant to become? Somehow, still, the world herself is not bounded by what we have made; her grandeur can still be felt. We c an still feel, though now feeling must be consciously developed and cultivated, and feeling is still part of a world process. Every abandoned building and empty lot can be seen by the I as an opportunity for a renovated house and a beautiful garden which reflect each other. The I does not need much to work with, for with our I we see possibilities of what the world could become.

With the first glimmering of true individuality, the very essence of the world is felt as love. This love is different than what we usually think of as love because it is creative and creative in full self-consciousness. This love does not spring forth out of nowhere, the world is its birthplace; but it can be sustained and developed only through developing the I.

In addition to the fragmented natural world that still inspires feeling and the possibility of creating beauty out of the I that is love, other world phenomena call us to awaken to this capacity of creating through love. There is the constant rhythm of day and night, the lunar cycle, and the yearly cycle of the sun. The significant aspect of these occurrences within which we are constantly immersed is that they are rhythmical. Rhythm is the essence of the world as feeling. Cultivating presence to these more encompassing world rhythms makes it possible to again feel rhythm where only inert things seem to exist.

The word *nature* comes from the Latin *natus*—to be born, becoming. Nature is not fixed, dead, immobile, inert. Not even rocks and earth are dead. The feeling of granite, its solidity and strength, is of a different quality than sandstone, which is soft and yielding. Any good architect knows that the feeling quality of the materials determines the feeling quality of the building. The I that creates is able to question the source of these qualities and to perceive that even rocks and dirt breathe, expand and contract in relation to the rhythms of seasons, take in or repel rain, hold or reflect the warmth of the sun, indicating that they too are part of the rhythms of the feeling world of nature. Paying attention to rhythm, both in the world and in individual life—the rhythm of sleeping and waking, the rhythm of work and rest, of concentration and relaxation—is central to developing toward individuality in relation to the world.

Purpose

In addition to the sense of I and the feeling perception of the rhythmic beauty of the world, individuality also consists of an active, enduring, pressing sense of purpose. In order to sense purpose that stems from our own individuality, all ideas of purpose that have been inculcated through past learning, education, family, religion, and society have to be located, examined, and recognized for what they are; they are what someone else wanted us to be. The kinds of purpose stemming from these sources may seem to be our own, may match our personality, and may seem to make life meaningful. However, when one reaches middle age, these ideas of purpose often come into question, as if something within has not ever been addressed, acknowledged, and honored.

When purpose makes itself felt, it does so in such a way that there is no doubt that purpose is far more than a subjective sensation. The field of its unfolding is the entire inner and outer world of the individual. The world often ceases to make sense, though it may have been entirely sensible for decades. Large changes in life-direction often present themselves. The danger here is always that the new-found direction may be yet another purpose defined by someone else. To change professions from being a lawyer to being a psychotherapist, for example, may be no more than switching from one institution to another. A partial alignment with purpose, as far as purpose is concerned, is an attempt to egotistically bend the individuality of purpose to suit one's own desire. Purpose involves the perfect alignment of inner impulse toward individuality with outer activity in the world. No compromises are possible.

Purpose goes together with glimmers of the sense of being an I and engagement with the rhythmic qualities of beauty in which world-feeling is felt. If one tries to insert purpose in the absence of these other two dimensions of individuality, there can be no alignment of the impulses toward change with what the world brings from its side. The lighting up of individuality as purpose thus takes the form of turmoil, chaos, darkness, the unknown, in which one seeks for what one does not know; it appears as profound dissatisfaction, even if, objectively seen, everything in one's life appears meaningful and comfortable. Psychology has long been aware of this threshold experience, has spoken of it as "mid-life" crisis, but always looks at this advent as a personal soul experience rather than as the world seeking to become conscious in us.

The soul intention of such a crisis in life, in which one feels that life can no longer be lived in the same manner as it had been, is to literally turn us inside out. This crisis indicates that now is the time we must begin to be the world's awareness rather than individuals who are aware of the world based upon our own needs and desires. Purpose, then, is never what we think it might be, as if we could control who we are. Thus, coming to the sense of purpose involves the act of continually releasing whatever and whoever we think we are. This act of releasing becomes a new habit, not merely something that is done until we find our "real" purpose. The paradoxical nature of purpose is that it is not a knowing but a doing. There is and must be consciousness in this doing of who we are, but it is never a consciousness that fixes itself into a completed idea.

Purpose does not seem to lie within us, but rather is revealed through our actions. Our actions take place in the world, and thus are on the outside rather than on the inside. Being turned inside out by the sense of purpose means beginning to become aware of this outside as if we were within it. Take, for example, even the most simple of actions, such as moving one's arm. Neither psychology nor physiology can adequately describe how this simple action takes place. From the viewpoint of psychology, all there is, at the very most, is an intention to move one's arm, an act of will to do so, and somehow, though immaterial, the idea works into the body, innervating the muscles, bringing about movement. From the viewpoint of physiology, it is all a matter of nerve centers, transmission from one part of the brain to another, and, similarly, innervation of the muscles of the body.

These feeble attempts at explanation are all based upon the assumption that something inside works toward the outside to produce an action in the world. If, on the other hand, I simply observe this action of my moving arm, suspending what I know from the past about cause and effect, and simply notice what is actually happening, I have to say that my arm is being moved not from inside but from outside. The inner, bodily feeling of this movement is the registering of the movement as a sensation. What, you are sure to ask, is outside causing my arm to move? The world. I reach for a cup across the table. The cup brings my arm toward it, not as a cause, producing an effect, movement, but as the purpose of my movement. This, I assure you, is no mere word game; it is a simple matter of observation.

We may further the observation. Say that I am thirsty, and my thirst causes me to move my arm across the table to reach the cup full of water. The movement now seems to originate with what is going on within me. The purpose seems to begin with me, and moving my arm seeks to fulfill that purpose. Impulse here is being confused with purpose. Impulse must be united with world in order to realize purpose. Whether instinct, impulse, need, fantasy, or idea, unless it finds its world relation, there is no purpose. And imposing any of these onto the world also does not accomplish what purpose concerns. Instinct can be enacted, impulse spent, need satisfied, fantasy acted out, idea put into action. None of these is the same as purpose, because with such imposition we are not acting individually but as an organism with instinct, a species with impulse, a general human being with need, an abstraction with idea. Thus, it is true that not every action in the world reveals purpose. It is also true, though, that every purpose is an action in the world. How is it possible to tell the difference, whether with regard to oneself or in viewing the actions of others?

With respect to oneself, action in the world can be experienced as purpose whenever it is part of the whole picture of the experience of being an I and sensing the feeling quality of the world. Action, then is creative rather than programmed, and feeling-filled rather than mechanical; that is to say, improvisation takes place, a play in the world, with the world as undivided partner.

These qualities can be observed in the actions of another person. A person may be doing a perfectly ordinary act, but it has rhythm, nuance, timing—an exteriority with interiority that unmistakably reveals itself as perfectly suited to the moment. One cannot help but imagine that, in moments such as these, the world leaps in joy.

In the absence of experiencing the creative, feeling dimensions of individuality, purpose cannot be felt as a positive quality of ongoing experience. Instead, it is felt as a longing and one goes in search of trying to find one's purpose. The absence of the sense of the I and of feeling interwoven with the fabric of world also produces the illusion that purpose is a bit of unknown information that can perhaps be supplied by the astrologer, the psychic, the psychotherapist. Purpose, however, is not of the same quality as information, for it is always in genesis, originating with each moment.

Living Individuality

The question now arises of how to sustain development of individuality, particularly in a civilization oriented toward making us forget there even is such a reality. Very often, individuality lived is something that one has to apologize for the next day. That is, we are for the most part not free enough from old conceptions that structure the world around us to sustain our side of creating a new world. Acting individually produces fear in those who live in sleepy comfort.

The full independence of the I, fully engaging with the world in its moment-by-moment coming into being, and uniting with the world as the realizing of purpose, can be taken to imply that if it were possible to live individuality one would not feel a need for other human beings. The very thought of not needing another person then may be enough to push individuality away if it begins to arise. It is quite so that from the viewpoint of individuality, another person is not someone to balance oneself, or someone who possesses what I do not, or a soulmate. I do not need another person to sustain a sense of myself, or to complete myself.

But, it is also the case that from the viewpoint of individuality, one stands in amazement alongside another. For of all that is in this world, nothing is more astounding than watching another develop out from egotism of soul, from egotism of emotion, from egotism of need toward individuality. To observe another working toward individuality as I am also trying to do, while respecting each as fully independent and always finding ways not to interfere, this is a true wonder. Thus, there is no difficulty at all in imagining that two people developing toward individuality would come into contact with each other.

Further, this contact would not be cool observation, but warm engagement, freely chosen. While one cannot direct another in the development of individuality, there is great joy in seeing the process occurring. The answer to what sustains the movement toward individuality can be found in this capacity to begin to observe another developing in such a direction. One then freely chooses to sustain that direction of development, not because another person is also moving this way and it is something to copy, but because of seeing that it is being done, because of seeing a new possibility. Nothing causes it, nothing supports it, nothing encourages it without the danger of becoming an outside force, which in all cases must be resisted. Movement toward individuality is a pure and free act of choice, an act which does not seek anything outside of itself. I cannot say that it makes me a better person, more whole, more complete, more comfortable, without that very claim removing the very essence of individuality.

As this process goes forward, it is necessary to begin to be aware of the things in the world that are detrimental to development in this direction. I do not avoid the world, but become more selective concerning which aspects of the world are chosen as avenues of experience. This choosing more likely takes the form of dropping

away things that bring forgetfulness of individuality, and of
being drawn to those expressions in the world which reveal individuality. Poetry expresses individuality, Rush Limbaugh expresses
individualism; television talk shows express egotism, an auto-
biography reveals individuality. Things that falsely promote individuality—advertising that says if you have the right pants, the
right car, the right toothpaste, then you are who you can be—
weaken the development of individuality.

Jacques Lusseyran, a remarkable individual who worked in the
French Resistance during the Nazi occupation of Paris, and who
was one of thirty survivors among two thousand Frenchmen incar-
cerated at Buchenwald, tells an important story of individuality.
First, all personal belongings were taken away, from clothes to wedding rings to pictures. Then each person was shaved—every hair
of the body. Each was systematically deprived of any distinctive-
ness. During this degrading process, many of the men began to
sob; anything that might indicate to an individual who he was had
been removed. Lusseyran was in a group of about thirty men who
went through this procedure on January 24, 1944. By March, every
one of the men except Lusseyran was dead. When their individualism was taken away, those who had not developed a sense of the
unassailability of the I were not able to survive.

Nothing can give us our sense of I. No one and nothing can
give this sense to another. Does this suggest that detachment is the
road to sustaining individuality?

Detachment is the way of compassion. Here, one more and
more comes to recognize the transitory character of everything—
that nothing is permanent, not even the mountains, the sky, the
sun, the stars. When one becomes capable of dissolving all attach-
ments, there is only what is spoken of as the Mind, not my mind,
but pure consciousness, with no trace of an I. If one has a glimmer
of such a state, then compassion develops, loving compassion,
which sees every aspect of the world going through the illusion of

taking the transitory as the permanent, and the suffering that
illusion engenders.

The way through the world, the way of the I, is ever so slightly
different than the path of compassion. Compassion and love are
so close that I suspect it is deceptive to imagine that they are
different in the way that two separate things are different from
each other. Compassion is based upon both an understanding of
and a connection with the *universal* spirit. The sense of the I as
love is based upon both an understanding of and a connection with
the *human* spirit. The two are in no way exclusive of each other.
The former has great comprehension of the universal; the latter,
great comprehension of the individual. The former sees the individual as valuable only to the extent that the cosmic spirit endows
it with content. The latter values the individual as such, and sees
the task of the individual spirit as key to transforming the world
through love.

In order to bring about such a transformation, the full freedom
of individuality must come to development. The egotism of individualism must yield to the freedom of individuality. The way of
compassion sees the passing of the earthly into the universal spirit
and finds liberation in this passing into the universal. The way of
the I also seeks liberation, but in a different direction, by transforming the material into the spiritual without loss of the
particularity of the material. This transformation cannot come
about without engagement, but engagement here has nothing to
do with gaining anything for oneself through this engagement.
Engagement is for the purpose of giving out love to the world; it
is individual love that transforms the world.

Love does not consist of something done by the I that is essentially outside it; love is the very substance and activity of the I.
Further, and this has been alluded to throughout this chapter but
must be repeated over and over, for it goes so contrary to the
assumptions of ordinary consciousness that it is almost immedi-

ately lost, the I is at the same time the activity of the entire universe encompassed by the awareness of the I. From this description of the I, which is not theory but can be at one and the same time knowledge and experience, it follows that living individuality is a matter of living ever increasingly into the world with immediate perception uncategorized by concepts from the past; it also follows that loving is the same as being ever more aware of the world as activity in which the I is engaged.

Being aware in this extended sense is a particular kind of meditative consciousness which, far from "navel gazing," is also an action awareness. One might imagine this action awareness as a polarity in which on one pole the sense of the I is centered at the place of the physical body, as a kind of nucleus. Then, the other pole is the sense of the I extended out to the limits of the stars, but continually varying, depending upon what the I centered at the place of the body is engaged in. As I sit here writing, there is the sense of the I, here, sitting on this chair; here I am, where I feel myself to be. At the same time, the I also consists of what I am doing at the moment, thinking and writing; it also consists of the visual appearance of this writing on the paper and of all that surrounds me. And all that surrounds me can expand or contract; it can be as narrow as the room I am in, or enlarge to the world outside, or, again, extend as far as the stars. This side of the polarity can be imagined as the range of the experience, not that the I has, but that is the I. Any movement of awareness is thus at the same time an action which changes the world.

One might well want to argue that the aspects of the world which are not within the immediacy of experience nevertheless continue to exist without this I. The stars and the sun and the moon and the earth and the cities and the country—all this seems completely independent of the I. First, it is necessary to recognize that in saying this, one has already slipped back into the I as no more than personal ego. Further, and while this may sound mystical, and it is not intended to be, would this supposedly independent world be there if there were no other I's in the world?

What I am trying to suggest is that the supposedly independent world is at every moment being supported in its being by the presence of every individual in the world, whether the individual has any inkling that this is the case or not. This way of imagining is based on the sense that the world is every moment in the act of coming to be. What we ordinarily think of as the "world out there" is the residue of past acts of creating, even past eons of the creating process. That world is in the process of dying, of passing gradually into inertness. That world is the world that is being used up, polluted, contaminated, exploited. It is the world that we human beings were given as the material substance with which to begin our own acts of creating; but instead of working with that given world and watching the creating processes occur there when they were still lively enough to be perceived, we used our creating powers to turn against that world.

This turn against the world, which began in earnest in the fifteenth century with the founding of natural science, cannot be called wrong or a mistake. Through natural science the creating acts possible for humans began to be discovered, and the discipline involved in learning to observe nature can be seen as exercises in developing toward the sense of the I. The schooling of consciousness required by natural science now needs, however, to be turned toward the I to make this form of creating conscious—rather than something used more or less irresponsibly to control rather than create the world.

Individuality and the Body

A great hindrance to developing the experience of individuality is found in the concept of the human body developed by the biological sciences and medicine. The capacity to transplant body organs, for example, makes it appear that the body is a collection of organs, more or less interchangeable from body to body. Our immediate experience of our own body and our perception of others in their bodily presence as utterly individual—not even identical twins are exactly alike in their incarnation—is defied by the ideas we now have of the body. These ideas are in fact so strong that they can be said to dull the capacity to actually perceive other humans in their true bodily individuality.

I want to briefly look at organ transplantation in the light of the question of individuality, in an attempt to dispel the ingrained but nonetheless unconscious thought we now live that if there is such a reality as individuality it does not reside within bodily existence. If this is indeed the case, the I is no more than a kind of ghost being, a spirit that uses the body.

What must be looked at in all forms of organ transplants, from blood transfusion to heart replacement, is the ever-present process of rejection. In the case of blood transfusion, for example, the blood received from another does not in fact become one's own blood. Rejection is constantly taking place, but at a rate such that by the time the rejection is completed, the individual's own blood has regenerated. The same is true for skin grafts. In instances of kidney or heart transplants, these organs also never become the substance and life of the body of the receiver. The basic idea is that the body of the receiver has to be tricked into living with a substitute organ as if it were one's own.

This necessary deception is achieved through the extraordinary feat of tricking the donated organ into acting as if it were still part of the donor while tricking the body of the receiver into living with this substitute. This feat is accomplished through administration of drugs (azathioprine, actinomycin-C, and corticosteroids) that paralyze the resistance of the body to receiving something foreign. In other words, receiving an organ implant is like getting a disease, and the body must be fooled into receiving this disease without rejecting it. Thus, the drugs also shatter the resistance to infection, and a balancing act has to be performed with the drugs, in which the disease that is the foreign organ is received and accepted but not the other kinds of infection.

An individual who has received a transplant thus lives a tenuous form of life with a necessary disease that allows life to continue. All of this points to the fact that we are individual, down to the cells of our body. No two hearts are alike, even in their anatomical construction. No two human bodies in the world are the same. The decision to receive a transplant involves much more than one can imagine. A transplant that does not just stand in for a while, but alters the integrity of the individual body, may make continued life possible, but it necessarily creates difficulties for the further development of the I, as our I is everywhere the same as the individuality of our body. I do not in any way imply that organ transplants are something that should not be done. However, regarding this utterly critical aspect of the process, that the unfolding of the I becomes far more difficult when living with an organ transplant, should not individuals faced with the decision of receiving an organ know what is at stake?

The importance of addressing the body in relation to individuality is that the I cannot be one-sidedly seen as spirit without body or soul without body. Further, our body is what makes it possible to tell whether or not individuality is being lived. It is not a matter of thinking that I am an individual, or of having an intuition that this is or is not the case; there are particular bodily sensations of individuality. The "I am an I" is also a sensing that this is so. These sensations are hard to describe; it is like being in tune, finding myself in places that are also in tune, that resonate with this sense of individuality. It is not necessary for thought or emotion to intercede; the body knows, and to know directly what the body knows is Wisdom, now conscious. When the conscious body senses that it is in the wrong place at the wrong time, it moves, makes changes, sometime very large life changes. These changes do not come about through emotional turmoil and ponderous consideration of whether we are living our destiny or not. Such convolutions occur only when what is sensed by the body is worked against rather than with. Then, we have to stop and think about it, go into therapy, look again at our past, and dull that Wisdom that presents a way into the future.

The way toward individuality is deceptively simple. When suffering is felt, it is time to move, to do something. The suffering is not something to be removed so that life can go on better in the circumstances in which one is living. Moving does not necessarily mean moving away or moving out. Moving means moving out of the fixed patterns of habit. All fear is the fear of doing, for doing may take away what one already has. And it does—it takes away the illusions that one has; it may take away the comfort that one has; it may take away the conceptions of who we think that we are, the ego sense of individualism that seems to give us our identity, but is not the I.

We do not move in order to feel better, have more, be more fulfilled, more happy, more satisfied. These things that we look for may or may not occur, for they are by-products rather than goals. They are all quite secondary to what can be discovered through developing the sense of the I-joy.

It is quite possible to feel joy while finding that the outer life is in many ways more difficult, more trying, more uncomfortable than what was lived before. The bodily sensation that tells us that we are at least moving toward the sense of individuality is joy. Nothing given from the outside can bring joy; it may bring pleasure, but not joy. We are always surprised by joy because this is living from the time current from the future and there are no concepts for joy.

3

THE SOUL
OF THE WORLD

D EVELOPING the sense of the I is at the same time coming
into a new kind of relationship with the world. I now
want to elaborate, in the context of the sense of the I, what is
encompassed by the word *world*. By world, I mean something different from our ordinary sense of the physical world, the Earth. I
also mean something different from the combination of the
Earth—with its mineral, plant, animal, and human life—and all
that has been developed in this place of Earth by human hands,
that is, culture and civilization. World as used here means the unity
of relationships between plant, animal, and human being on the
one hand, and Earth and cosmos on the other—not just in an
external way, but according to the shared characteristic of soul. I
am using the term *world* in a sense similar to that which has been
used through a long tradition concerned with the Soul of the
World, she who is also called Sophia.

The Essenes, the Gnostics, the practitioners of Hermeticism,
monastic Christian mysticism, alchemy, and ceremonial magic, the
Cathars, the Rosicrucians, the Kabbalists, the School of Chartres,
and in modern times, Russian Sophiology, depth psychology,
Theosophy, and Anthroposophy—all have placed the World Soul
at the center of their transformational activity. In all ages and in all
places, an unending partnership of the human, the divine, and the
world has been declared, proclaimed, and protected through the
presence of the Sophia. Her creating and mediating activity—

under such names as Isis, Sophia, Wisdom, Shekinah, Achamoth, World Soul, Athena, Alchymia, Spenta Armatii, Black Virgin, Mary, Eternal Feminine—has always looked toward the future birth of creation into the cosmos of love. The present time, I believe, signals the genesis of this birth. New soul capacities are ready to be cultivated, practiced, and brought into practical action, capacities needed to fulfill our part in the destiny of Sophia.

The World Soul

The complex and varied centrality of Sophia in the traditions mentioned has been masterfully and comprehensively put forth by Caitlin Matthews in *Sophia, Goddess of Wisdom: The Divine Feminine from Black Goddess to World Soul*.[1] I do not intend to summarize her work, however, and in fact will take a somewhat different approach. Rather than approaching Sophia through cataloging her iconography throughout time, I will orient here solely toward deepening the insight that working toward individuality is indivisibly also working toward the Soul of the World. Once this inseparable tandem can be more fully felt as an actuality and not mere theory, it will be possible in following chapters (especially chapters 9 and 10) to bring forth some of the ways this new comprehensive reality is seeking to be realized.

Sophia may be characterized by a certain hiddenness that is not concealed behind something, but hidden precisely through the way she is revealed as the world. When we observe the world in all its varied physical manifestations, something not apparent nonetheless pervades everything—namely, that all this multiplicity of plant, animal, and human world is a totality, a unity; it all works together. Further, this totality that all works together does so in relation with all the other planets, the Moon, the Sun, and the constellations of the zodiac. And there is yet another hiddenness—this unity binds to itself the particularity of every human soul in its individuality.

All of this, considered together, is what is indicated by Sophia, Wisdom, the Soul of the World.

Beginning in the way we have, with the question of the soul of individuality, inevitably takes us to the Soul of the World. The two are inseparable. Since, however, individuality is not something that is completed, but is coming to be, the first thing we can say concerning the World Soul is that she also is coming to be. Sophia differs from any other goddess images—she is incomparable with the Great Mother or with Gaia because she is a spiritual out-pouring that is from the future, not the past. Sophia is a new-coming, not a has-been. While images of Sophia can be found in all times, these images are intimately bound up with a sense of what is coming to be. Sophia myths are not archeological, looking backward, nor timelessly eternal, a static given, but rather eternally teleological.

I am dealing here with things difficult to imagine and do not want to succumb to the easy resolution of putting it all inside and speaking of the Sophia within, or of putting it all outside and thus turning the difficulties over to theology. So a word is needed about the kind of imagination at work. The traditions cited above, which list I will abbreviate by calling it the Hermetic tradition, consisted of freelance lovers of Wisdom. These perpetual researchers were unencumbered by dogma and also knew that imagination is not only inside but also outside. The point of view put forward in this work follows this same folly. I place myself in the tradition that has always been concerned with approaching the future not out of prophecy, prediction, or New Age optimistic expectations, but from a real and substantial time current of soul coming to us from what can be.

The world cannot be directly perceived as a unified whole, how-ever inviting and appealing such an idea may be. Nonetheless, unity is not just an abstract idea without foundation in the perceived world. In Proverbs, Sophia herself speaks a picture of this quality of unity:

> The Lord knew me at the beginning of his ways; before he created anything. I was installed from eternity. When the deeps were not yet in existence, I was already born; when the springs were not flowing with water, before the mountains were set upon their foundations, before the hills, I was born. When he had not yet made the Earth and what is upon it, nor the mountains of the surface of the Earth, when he prepared the heavens, I was there. I was there when he measured the deep, when he fixed the clouds above, when he made firm the springs of the deep, when he set a limit to the sea and the waters so that they should not overstep his command, when he laid the foundation of the Earth. (8: 22–29)

The unknown, invisible soul quality of unity is present from the beginning. She is the plan of creation, its idea, its Wisdom. Wisdom further consists of a unity of three different and nonetheless related and interpenetrating qualities. We must be able to imagine three inseparable moments to the act of creating: the potential, the ideal, and the actual. Wisdom is the Mother of all, the potential; the ideal unity of the all is the Daughter, and the actuality of the all is the Holy Soul.

Bernardus of Silvestris, advisor to Bernard of Clairvaux who was responsible for the construction of Chartres Cathedral, an earthly temple of Sophia, developed the picture of these three qualities of Sophia in the year 1147. His work *Cosmographia* can be translated as "The All-encompassing Unity of the World." The cathedral was actually built according to these three principles, and thus is a visible expression of Sophia herself, not just a building honoring Sophia. That is to say, Chartres Cathedral is an embodiment of Sophia. Chartres Cathedral is a place of the future, not a monument of the past.

Sophia is thus spoken of as the Holy Trinosophia, an undivided unity of three qualities of soul activity. We may ask how the individual soul relates to this unity, for as stated above, the individuality of the human soul is indeed bound to this unity. Since our interest centers on the question of individuality in relation to the world, this relation is central.

Bernardus of Silvestris also grappled with this question. He first describes the reflection of the Holy Trinosophia within the individual soul as the capacity to imagine in wholes, which he calls reason. Reason for him does not mean thinking or analyzing, moving from part to part, nor does it mean imagination as looking at inner pictures. Bernardus means the ability to have an inner sense of the inner qualities of outer things as existing in relation with one another. This is the Wisdom of the human soul, the Mother aspect.

The second capacity, undivided from this first ability, Bernardus calls imagination. By imagination he means our intuitive sense that everything is in relation to everything else must be brought forth actively through the making of images that reflect our sensing of unity. For Bernardus, the soul is first a receptive quality of sensing unity; this must be actively taken up in the production of images reflecting this unity. Say, for example, the moment comes when the windows of Chartres Cathedral are to be the focus of consideration. Soul activity must be directed toward picturing the windows, in their individuality and particularity, as reflecting the sense of the whole. We can also imagine the work involved in trying to live this way in all spheres of life. If we want to plant something in the garden, for instance, then we must actively imagine how a particular plant relates to all of the plants of the garden, how the garden relates to the rest of the landscape, the landscape to the region, the region to the whole geography, the geography to the rest of the Earth, the rest of the Earth to the cosmos. Nothing is done haphazardly or out of a concept of what is "needed" without consideration of the whole; this is true imagination, the Daughter aspect of the human soul.

The third activity of soul, undivided from reason and imagination, Bernardus calls memory. Memory here is deeper than the usual sense of a capacity to recall the personal past. Memory means that the human being is itself a recollection of the whole of creation. This recollection of the whole is expressed as the form and activity of the human body. The body is itself the visible expression of soul. The head in its roundedness, for example, remembers or reflects the unity of Wisdom and is the temple of reason, with the senses being like windows of the temple. The region of the heart remembers in the human body the activity of imagination, the active force of synthesizing. The region of the limbs remembers the necessity of action in the world in a way that always re-forms the unity of the whole. Memory is thus really an abbreviated description, in the individualized human body, of the unity and activity of the whole.

Given such magnificent pictures of the completeness of the World Soul, both in its structure and in its action, the interesting question is why the world does not seem to function in this ideal way. We can get a feeling for what the world would be like if it did. In a word, everything would be in harmony. Every part of the world would function as part of the whole; it would not exactly be Paradise, for constant effort of reason, imagination, and memory would be required. But this effort would constantly be rewarded with the direct experience that nothing works in isolation. Surprisingly, that the world does not function in this way is also due to the nature of Sophia herself.

The aspect of Sophia that explains why it has been possible to turn away from her and act as if unity is no more than an abstract idea concerns the particular nature of the binding of the individual soul with the Soul of the World. The Russian Sophiologist, Vladimir Soloviev, wrote in about 1884 of this particular quality.

> Why does not this union of the divine beginning [spoken above as the potential], with the world soul [spoken above as the ideal], and

the resultant birth of the world organism [the actual]—why does not this union take place at once? . . . The full answer to this question is contained in one word; that word is *freedom*. By a free act of the world soul, the world united by it [the world soul] fell apart within itself into the multitude of elements warring among themselves; by a long series of free acts that whole multitude must make peace among themselves and be reconciled.[2]

This act of freedom is necessary for the evolution of that aspect of the World Soul bearing self-consciousness, the individual soul, to come into its own. The World Soul has undergone the long process of evolution, a kind of fall from unity, in order that this unity might be again fulfilled, now fully consciously. Restoring the World Soul to its unity thus becomes weighted on the side of the development of fully conscious individual soul life: the task of human beings in the destiny of Sophia.

Sophia in Myth and Legend

Let us now look at how this complex character of Sophia is expressed in the stories of Sophia. Here, we have in picture form, with some additional key elements, what Soloviev strains to say in discursive language. The Gnostic story "Pistis Sophia," in particular, pictures the fall of Sophia.[3] "Pistis Sophia" means "Ever-Faithful Wisdom." The story begins with the existence of a primal pair, Depth and Silence. Depth and Silence bring forth, or emanate, thirty Aeons, levels of manifestation, archetypal forms. The archetypal manifestation of the thirtieth level is Sophia. Sophia falls in love with the light of Depth and desires to unite with this light. Her desire, however, confuses her. She moves toward what seems to be the light, but she in fact is moving toward an equally brilliant light in the region of Chaos. She is thrown into Chaos, where she encounters other beings, the Demiurge and the rulers, and a being described as having a lion's face and filled with pride. In this region of Chaos, Sophia suffers every psychic torment imaginable—fear, anxiety, passion, terror, despair, sadness, sorrow. Out of the psychic torrent raging through her, the elements of earth, water, air, and fire form and condense into the Earth. The lion-faced being filled with pride also forms elements of earth, water, air, and fire, which also condense into Earth. From the pleroma, the Fullness, Depth and Silence see the travail of Sophia. Jesus is united with the Christ and enters into Chaos to retrieve Sophia. But, Sophia is reluctant to depart from Chaos; she is filled with compassion for Earth, because she knows the effects of the condensation created by the lion-faced being filled with pride. She divides herself in two. The heavenly Sophia is returned to Depth and Silence, and the earthly Sophia must wait and be a reminder to the human soul to strive toward the development of unity.

In this myth we again are made aware of the threefold nature of Sophia. There is the heavenly Sophia, the Wisdom of the world that is the potential of the unity of the all. And there is the Sophia who remains in the realm of Chaos. The third Sophia is the Sophia manifested as the creation of the elements which condense into Earth, for she cannot be separated from what she creates. This sense of Earth is not the Earth in its material substance alone, but Earth in all of its qualities—the movement of light, color, and shadow, the depth of things in their particularities, the healing qualities of herbs, the particular qualities of the animals, such as the swift-moving legs characterizing the cougar, the flowing back of the deer. The Earth as material substance is the creation of the lion-faced being filled with pride. We might think of him as the archetypal literalist, the sense of the world as inert substance, used by plants and creatures, and exploited by human beings as a source of resources.

An additional insight given by this myth is that not only is the nature of the Sophia threefold, but these three aspects are here shown to be separated—which is a way of saying that the unity of all of creation was broken. The act through which this unity separates is the free act of Sophia. First, there is the act of her wanting to return to the light of Depth; this indicates that Sophia was not conscious of her own destiny as mediatrix between the divine and the earthly, that she is simultaneously the divine and the earthly. An evolution of her being is necessary for her to become conscious of her destiny; but this must be brought about by the evolution of the individual soul, which is a dimension of the World Soul, the dimension of consciousness. The free act of Sophia, however, is her choice to remain trapped in the region of Chaos, at the center of the Earth, in the darkness of the underworld. The separation of threefold Sophia into the heavenly, earthly, and underworld Sophia means that the unity that is the Soul of the World is something that now has to be accomplished through the efforts and development of human individuality oriented not to our own development alone, but for the sake of the world.

The image of this future coming-together of heavenly, earthly and underworld Sophia is the image of the Sophia of the Apocalypse. The picture is given in chapter 12 of the book of Revelation: "And there appeared a great wonder in heaven; a woman clothed with the Sun, and the Moon under her feet, and upon her head a crown of twelve stars." Literalists read the Apocalypse as the story of the end of the world. From the point of view we are taking, it is rather the picture of the formation of the new world of the unity of the cosmic soul, the earthly soul, and the individual soul, now in full consciousness. The Sophia of the Apocalypse is the image of the unity of the three aspects of Sophia. That she stands with the Moon under her feet means that the complete sphere of the earthly realm, which includes the regions from the underworld up to the Moon, is brought into the unity that is Sophia. That she is clothed with the Sun means that all of the regions of earthly life become luminous in the unity of Sophia. And that she is crowned with twelve stars means that she encompasses all of the heavenly realm, to the outermost twelve constellations of the zodiac.

An even more significant attribute of this image of Sophia is that these three realms when brought together are all expressed through qualities of rhythm: the heavenly rhythm of the Sun moving through the constellations of the zodiac; the earthly rhythm of the Sun of day and night; and the rhythm of the cycle of the Moon. This complete dominance of rhythm says that the unity of the Soul of the World has to do with the development of the capacity to see all things in their activity, motion, mobility, ever-changing movement. The kind of consciousness that is capable of doing this, we have described as the activity of the I.

A contemporary freelance lover of Wisdom who wished to remain anonymous, but who has many published works, including the extraordinary *Meditations on the Tarot,* has received a prayer to Sophia. It might be good to place this prayer before us now as a way of recollecting all that has been said concerning Sophia up to this point. Reflection on this prayer can be a preparation for the next task: developing the individual soul to the point of consciousness that is a soul consciousness, the I that can be the activity of uniting itself with the Soul of the World.

The Our Mother Prayer

Our Mother, thou who art in the darkness of the underworld,
May the memory of the holiness of thy name shine forth,
May the breath of the awakening of thy kingdom warm
     the hearts of all homeless wanderers,
May the resurrection of thy will enliven eternal faithfulness
     even unto the depths of corporeal substance.
Receive this day the living remembrance of thee from
     human hearts,
Who implore thee to forgive the debt of forgetting thee,

And are ready to fight against the temptation in the world
which has led thee to existence in the darkness,
That through the Deed of the Son the immeasurable pain of
the Father be stilled,
Through the freeing of all beings from the tragedy of thy
withdrawal,
For thine is the homeland, and the all-bestowing greatness,
and the all-merciful grace, for all and everything in the
circle of all.[4]

Prayer is perhaps the most intimate form of conversation. I do not take prayer to be an act of submission, for this would be to violate the character of the I. The I freely chooses to relate with soul and spiritual realms as dimensions of the world, but it does not create a separate realm of gods, goddesses, and spirits as the way to avoid individual responsibility.

Freeing Sophia from the underworld requires, first, that she be addressed. The world must be addressed as a living being. She is not known to our ordinary everyday consciousness; this consciousness must radically change if we are to enter into her depth. Entering the underworld refers to the transition from a materialistic point of view to a soul point of view. A darkening of ordinary consciousness is required. The Black Madonna, retrieved from beneath Chartres Cathedral and enthroned above it, images this change of consciousness.

The first petition to Sophia indicates the direction consciousness moves to make connection with her. Memory here is memory in the sense depicted by Bernardus Silvestris. The meeting with Sophia first occurs as the sense of our own body as an individual unity of the form and activity of the world. We first remember her not by retrieving the past, but by giving attention to the wholeness, the holiness, of the individual body and the unity of head, heart, and action.

Re-membering the soul qualities of the body brings forth another petition, that our alienation from her kingdom awaken the capacity of imagination centered at the place of the heart. This awakening is first felt as the sense that every human being, insofar as the memory of unity of ourselves as individual expressions of the whole is not realized, is homeless. What we do or make or accomplish ultimately will not make sense without seeing through the heart.

What is the will of the Soul of the World? Is it not to enliven the soul sense of the world, to redeem the literalistic view of the Earth, to bring about through the individual soul the realization that everything is in soul? The very thought of this possibility inspires an adherence to what is not yet, but can be. Faithfulness, in this instance, is not to the God above, but to the depths of the body, of inner life. This faithfulness does not abandon the substance of the world but goes ever more deeply into it.

The re-membering of the Soul of the World is an act of the individual imagination of the heart. It is an act of love, fully conscious and individual love. The movement of the heart seeks to balance our excessive concentration, interest, and involvement in our own concerns, our tendency to act as if the world were no more than a setting within which we play out our own self-interests. An imagination of the heart requires constant attention, for without that nearly everything in the world is oriented toward diverting attention from the sense of the whole.

The deed of the Son refers to the Second Coming. But the Second Coming need not be taken as the end of the world. The Second Coming here refers to the descent of the Christ into the realm of Chaos to bring Sophia back to the pleroma, as spoken of in the Pistis Sophia myth. This coming also refers to the selfless kind of love, the development of true individual capacity to love, that is needed to strive toward the potential of the unity of all. The Father is in pain because his equal is lost; the interior sense, the soul sense of the world is lost. We begin to be freed from the tragedy of this loss when we begin to live in and live with the sense of soul. A fully conscious, individual sense of the I as creating the unity of the all is the first step of a return to the homeland of the all in the circle of all.

Sophia and the Grail

A central story picturing the development of the sense of the I, and the intimate relation between the I and the Soul of the World is the Grail legend. Many themes I take up in later chapters are foreshadowed in this legend, which is a story not of the past but of our time and of the future. I will here consider only some images from the first part of this legend as told in Wolfram von Eschenbach's *Parzival*, written about the twelfth century. The work itself tells us that it pictures something from the future, even though the characters are kings and queens and knights, along with many most extraordinary women.

The pictures of the Grail story are said to have come from a reader of the stars named Flegitanis. This does not mean that the work originates in astrology, but rather through someone who was able to see in the movement of the constellations the movement, the evolution, of the Soul of the World. That is to say, this work is a work not of prediction, but of an imagination of the gradually developing unity potential between cosmos, world, and individual soul. This first part of the legend, in particular, can be worked with as showing the practical activity, the work, involved in coming to experience the Soul of the World through the development of individuality.

In *Parzival*, we are first given a picture of the hero's father, Gamuret. Gamuret's father has died, and his land is given to the eldest son, who is a brother of Gamuret. Gamuret's brother is generous and offers Gamuret land and wealth. Gamuret refuses this generosity, not out of malice or bitterness, but because, he says, he has a burning, a passion in his heart. He does not know what this longing is about, but decides that he must find out, and feels that he must leave behind all that he has been given from the past in order to pursue this unknown longing. He starts on a journey to the East, with the intention of serving the greatest warrior in the world, Baruch of Baghdad.

Gamuret does not just give up wealth and land. He relinquishes the world as he knows it, which encompasses all he has learned, his family, his civilization and culture, his religion, his own way of knowing. "East" here signifies the unknown, the mysterious. Giving up our sense of the past means putting our ego into question, ceasing to live by what we receive from the past, and entering the unknown. If we can, but for a moment, put aside our accustomed ways of approaching the world, which have to do with what we have been given from the past, we will feel what Gamuret felt, a passionate longing, but for what?

In his quest, Gamuret first engages in a battle at the castle of Petalamunt, which is under siege. He falls in love with the queen of that castle, Belekane, a beautiful black woman. The name Belekane means "Pelican," a name that reverberates with the alchemical picture of the pelican who wounds herself, pierces her own heart, in order to feed her offspring. Belekane is our first picture of the Soul of the World in this story. She is a dark, unknown figure, like Sophia in the underworld. Gamuret marries Belekane, but does not stay long with her; for the fire still burns in his heart, and he must have more of lady adventure. Belekane is abandoned, a picture of the Soul of the World abandoned and in sorrow. Gamuret does not realize that he is in need of soul.

Then, Gamuret marries a second beautiful woman, Herzeleide, a name that means "Heart's Sorrow." From this union Parzival is born, though Gamuret leaves again, before he knows of the pregnancy.

Gamuret subsequently is killed in battle, in the service of the Baruch of Baghdad. He is killed by an act of sorcery. The diamond on his helmet is secretly dipped in an alchemical preparation of goat's blood, an elixir so hot that it can soften a diamond's hardness. Thus, when Gamuret goes into battle, his source of strength is drained and he is killed. This image tells us of the deficiency in Gamuret. He confuses the longing in his heart with passion. He does not see that it is a longing for soul, but takes his longing literally, as a passion for some unknown but literal thing. His clear, diamond-like vision is thus flawed. He can be overcome by his weakness, the heat of passion. Thus, the alchemical potion is able to bring his downfall.

When we give up what we have been given from the past and face the unknown future, there is the strong likelihood that the longing felt will be taken literally. We go in search of some actual thing that would seem to satisfy the longing—a new marriage, job, career, religion, education, home. All of this literal searching is the attempt of the ordinary ego to reinstate itself as knowing oneself by knowing what one has. Leaving the ego sense of ourselves is a constant task, not something that once done is then completed. And without the sense of soul, there is really no satisfying of longing literalized.

Upon learning of the death of Gamuret, Herzeleide mourns, and after a time takes her son Parzival away from the world of wealth, culture, and civilization. They establish a home far away in the woods. She does not want Parzival to know anything of the world, anything of knighthood; for she knows that if he did he would become a knight and leave her, and risk being killed as her husband was. Again we are given pictures of leaving the past, of emptying the ego of its capacities of acting from what is imagined, remembered, and known from the past.

One day, while young Parzival is hunting birds with a bow and arrow in the woods, a brilliant flash of light appears. He thinks this is God, for his mother has told him that God is light. What he actually sees is the shining armor of knights, who laugh at Parzival's foolishness. When he learns what knights do, Parzival knows he wants to be a knight in the court of Arthur. He leaves his mother to go in search of knighthood. His mother, most reluctant to let him go, dresses him as a fool and gives him a broken-down horse to ride; she is calculating that such a foolish-looking boy will never be taken seriously. Then she tells him a story concerning how to treat women—which Parzival hears, not as a story, but as literal instruction. This image of Parzival as the fool is the clue to how the Soul of the World must be approached. We must become aware of the foolishness of our longings, realize that no literal thing can satisfy longing, and nevertheless not give up the longing; this is what Parzival must come to realize, a step away from the ego sense of self toward individuality.

Parzival leaves on his quest to become a knight. He first comes to a tent in the woods. He enters the tent and sees a beautiful woman, Jeschute, sleeping, naked. He wakes her, takes her ring and brooch, eats the food that is there, and leaves. He takes the ring and brooch because this is part of the story his mother told him about how to treat women. When we first approach the realm of the soul—for example, when we become interested in our dreams—our first interest is in what we can take from this realm: What is there in my dreams that is sparkling and glittering that can tell me something about myself? This is an ego move in relation to the soul. The literal ego has no sense of serving soul, only of taking from her. Such a way of approaching the soul realm brings harm to this realm. When Jeschute's husband returns he thinks that she has been unfaithful to him, which she was not. He punishes her severely, making her ride in tattered clothes on a broken-down horse, the soul in exile. Jeschute is a picture of the individual soul, of how we mistreat our soul, making access to World Soul more difficult.

Parzival rides on, oblivious to the injury he has caused. He comes to a second woman, Sigune, who sits in the middle of a clearing in the woods, holding her dead husband. This image of Sigune—the way she sits, her faithfulness to her husband, her silent, waiting posture, there in the midst of the world—this is a Pietà. This suffering, abandoned World Soul is not the Sophia of the underworld or the heavenly Sophia, but the Sophia of Earth. Parzival approaches her, not out of compassion, but out of curiosity. It is as if, seeing the dead knight, he gets a glimmer of what could happen to him. His interest is his self-interest. This woman, to whom Parzival is related though he does not know that, tells Parzival his name. His mother never had told him his name, but always called him "Sweet Son."

The name Parzival means "through the middle," which tells us of his destiny. His task does not concern a spiritual quest that leaves behind the actual world, nor does his task concern turning away from the world to enter into the interior soul life. He is destined for the Grail, which is to serve the Soul of the World. In the course of the story, Parzival encounters Sigune two more times. Each time his attitude toward her is dramatically different. It changes from curiosity, to respect, to reverence—a transition from ego to I.

There is yet a third woman. Parzival, still dressed as a fool, rides into a village. Cunneware sees him and laughs. Cunneware had taken a vow never to laugh until she saw someone worthy of the highest of honor. She sees something of the true individuality of Parzival. Her guardian, Sir Kay, strikes her when she laughs. Parzival sees this happen, but does nothing about it at that moment. He does, however, realize in that brief moment that she is beaten because of him. It is his first awareness that there is a binding of soul and individuality.

The last of the women figures of the Grail story I will draw attention to here is Condwiramurs, the wife of Parzival. Her name means "bringer of love." When Parzival marries her, it looks as though there will be a repetition of what happened with Gamuret. After a short time with Condwiramurs, Parzival becomes restless. The source of his restlessness, however, is different from that of his father. He remembers his mother and desires to go and see her. He does not know that she died out of grief when he left. He leaves to return to her but instead comes to the Grail castle, and there has his first encounter with the Grail itself. This encounter is an entry into the realm of imagination—not personal imagination, but the imagination of the world. But Parzival is not awake to what he experiences; his imagination is not a fully awake, conscious imagination. He is expelled from the Grail castle, and goes wandering.

All of these pictures of the early adventures of Parzival are preparations for what is to come, the development of his capacity to serve the Grail, the Soul of the World. All of the women are Sophia figures, educators bringing about the transformation from the ego to the I. A major characteristic of all of these Sophia figures is their radical receptivity. I do not take these figures to represent the plight of women, nor do I take Parzival to be an image of the masculine. The story has to do with the relation between ego and soul, with the transformation from ego to I, from getting to giving, and with the development of the active capacity of conscious love, the substance of the I, which cannot be separated from the Soul of the World. The radical receptivity of Sophia shows the way to a new kind of love. Receptivity is not passivity; it brings about radical change.

The Membrane of the Elements

In the "Pistis Sophia," Sophia brings soul qualities to Earth as a condensing of the elements of earth, water, air, and fire. The individual human body is also a condensing of these elements. The elements are not substances; they are not what we ordinarily know as earth, water, air, and fire. The first systematic teaching about the

elementary constituents of the world was given in the fifth century
B.C., by Empedocles, who described them as the dynamic conditions that bring about the forming of all things.

The elements are dynamic qualities that are both outer and
inner at the same time. According to the alchemists, every individual thing consists of a particular combination of the elements;
every single thing consists of earth, water, air, and fire, as does the
totality of things. A stone has a preponderance of the earth element, but the other three qualities are also involved. Water has a
preponderance of the water element, but that it can solidify into
ice shows that the earth element is involved; that it can evaporate
shows that the air element is also an aspect; and that it can change
from one state to another is due to the fire element.

The human body is also a totality of the elements, making the
elements like a membrane through which the individual body is in
constant connection with the body of the world. The binding of
the individual soul with the Soul of the World is related to the
complex functioning of the elements.

Of the four elements, earth and fire are primarily outer qualities; water and air are primarily inner qualities. Fire is outer
movement, which can be imagined as the light, the liveliness, the
glow, the radiance of matter. Fire is not heat, but it does bring
about the quality of warmth. Earth is outer form, the boundedness
of each thing, the solidity, firmness, shape that belongs to each
thing. Earth is not substance, but brings about the primary quality of substance. Water is the inner form of things, characterized
by a sense of flow, fluidity, depth, moistness, and the relating quality that links one thing to another; it is not the substance water,
but a quality of fluidity present in all things. Air is the inner movement of things, the quality of expansiveness. When we look at an
object, it has a certain shape and form that can be seen from the
outside. The same shape and form can also be imagined as proceeding from the inside of the object, working toward the outside.

Depending on how we look at a thing, we can see it as a contraction into a form or an expansiveness from within outward.

A sense of the elements is important because it gives us pictures that help develop the capacity to experience the particularity of things that are each also expressions of the total unity of everything. Sophia, the unity of the all, is not to be understood as a dissolving of the particularity and multiplicity of the world, the many becoming one, but rather as the many as one.

The elements are also important because they reflect the creating activity of Sophia. Through the four elements, the visible world is inseparably linked with the interior qualities of soul. We could say that Sophia is imagining the world, and the image that she imagines is the body of the world forming through the elements. The body of the world is the visible image of Sophia. The individual soul imagines the human body; the human body, forming through the elements, is the visible image of the soul. Both the body of the world and the individual human body are constantly being created through the imagining activity of soul. Since, however, the same elements are involved in both the world and the individual, we are led to say that the Soul of the World expresses herself in one way as imagining the world and in another way as imagining the individual human body. Sophia creating the body of the world as a potential unity could be spoken of as Sophia imagining her destiny. Sophia creating the individual human body could be spoken of as Sophia imagining that this destiny is to be brought about in the freedom of conscious activity.

The elements cannot be imagined as qualities of space, though they lead to the existence of such qualities. In their primary, originating action, the elements are time activities—the way in which time shapes itself into the form, structure, and action of the world. We usually imagine time in terms of space—a before and after, or yesterday, today, and tomorrow, or the position of the hands on a clock, or the movement of the Sun. The elements as time are pure activity, motion, and mobility, differentiated in four different but related ways.

The loss of the capacity to experience this creating activity of time brings about the feeling that the I is separate from the world, despite the fact that the I is really time as it is coming to be. When it began to imagine the world primarily in terms of space rather than time, the self also lost its awareness as a time being. I want now to explore the implications of that separation. For a long time, this separation was needed and enabled the making of a world that made sense in terms of past, present, and future. The making of this kind of world, however, has now reached a turning point, a crisis requiring the development of new modes of imagining both self and world.

4

TIME, LOVE, AND
THE SOUL

On August 6, 1945, our sense of time, which had been wobbly since about the fifteenth century, lost its direction. The flow of time in a stream of continuity that made possible building on tradition from the past, experiencing the present, and moving toward the future was so severely interrupted that it has become harder and harder to make sense of the world. It is as if the event of the first atomic bomb brought about a rupture in the time stream. Since then we have been improvising, based on fragmented memories of the way the world used to work.

A deep feeling of nausea, first articulated by Sartre in his description of what it really means to be isolated, tells us that this game of acting like time is the same as it always was will not work anymore. The great cosmic instruction manual on how to live in relation with the universe went up in the conflagration in Japan. A remarkable event, the bomb. On one hand, the explosion was a very literal event. On the other hand, the explosion of the bomb is an epiphany—the appearance of a new god that questions the power of former divinities, a god capable of creating the capacity to destroy not only the Earth, but perhaps even a greater part of the galaxy. The god is each of us; the bomb, a declaration of independence from the divine worlds.

Those scientists and technicians who created the bomb seem to be very clever people indeed. But to invent a thing such as the atomic bomb, besides the intelligence required, three soul qualities are also required. First, there must be absolute doubt that anything exists of a soul or spirit nature in the world. In order for such doubt to prevail, atheism is not necessary. I imagine that many of these people believed in God; but it is impossible to imagine that they directly experienced the invisible, unknown factor of soul in the world. Second, there must be an absolute capacity of hatred. This capacity, further, could not be expressed in a direct manner, for then it would be an overwhelming emotion resulting in immediate action rather than the cool objective discipline needed to make an object embodying the most intense hatred imaginable. Third, there must be absolute fear of others. This kind of fear is necessary in order to imagine that such a device can be directed toward others who are like oneself, human beings whom it is possible to come to know as individuals.

These qualities of consciousness are what we must try to examine in ourselves, for these scientists simply expressed in clear form the condition of the modern soul in relation to the world. For the individual soul to have developed in this direction, the world as the place of soul would have to have been already obscured and forgotten for a long time. Now, more than fifty years after the explosion of the bomb, we see these same characteristics of doubt, hatred, and fear exploding in the world. A new kind of violence characterizes the modern world. Terrorism can be seen in relation to these characteristics of the modern soul; so can street violence, drive-by shootings, mass murders, cases of individuals walking into office buildings and coolly taking out a gun and killing seven or eight people. This new violence is not characterized by passion and loss of control, but rather by coolness and calculation; we might even call it scientific, technological violence.

We cannot simply say that the bomb is the product of science and technology, and that the scientists and technologists are to be blamed, but not the rest of us. These ways of knowing and controlling the world are no more than the extension of the kind of consciousness we all now live, and it may be time to take responsibility for the independent life of consciousness. This independence centers around the capacities of self-consciousness. Self-consciousness has developed in humanity as a whole to such a point that we now experience ourselves as separate from the world around us, and this separateness makes possible using what is around us to create our own world. Human creating has now proceeded so far that it is nearly impossible to find any sector of the world untouched by the act of human making.

A primary characteristic of our current way of making the world is that Wisdom, Sophia, has no part; that is, what we make of the world does not first look to the Wisdom in the arrangement and functioning of the already given world, but quickly turns its back on her. We neglect the Soul of the World as the unknown factor that makes the multiplicity of the world also a unity and gives us the feeling that we live in a world, not simply amongst a multitude of separate things. The result is the making for ourselves of a world without soul.

The desire to experience both unity and multiplicity at the same time lives deeply within everyone. In our daily life in the world, multiplicity now reigns. We identify ourselves with each separate thing that engages us—work, family, relationship, parenting, and all the rest—with no feeling for how it all works as a whole, yet assume that it must. Constant movement from one isolated activity to another produces a need for turning away from the world to experience moments of unity—a weekly hour at church, another at the office of the therapist or counselor, meditation practices, the quest for wholeness of body, soul, and spirit. These practices of turning away from the world may nourish the individual soul and spirit, but the world does not seem thereby to also be replenished.

But a sacred center does exist that can bring the inner and the outer together; this sacred center is the I. Having explored this center in relation to individuality, and having also presented pictures of the Soul of the World, we can now work to make their relation more clear.

Time and the Soul

What is the relation between the individual soul and the World Soul? Depth psychology has done much to convince us that the individual psyche, or soul, consists of far more than what we call the ego, the ordinary but highly restricted sense of the I. As such, it constitutes a profound religious endeavor; through finding the sacred within, it makes a link back to sacred beings. Soul, however, which is the mainstay of all depth psychologies, is always related by them to the past, whether the individual past or the collective past.

Depth psychology begins by showing that phenomena such as dreams and pathologies demonstrate that there are regions of soul life of which we are quite unaware. Then these regions of soul life are said to be patterned by either A) what has happened to us in our own individual past, or B) more deeply, by the patterns and behaviors of gods, goddesses, spirits, daimones, expressed in the great mythologies of the world, but now living in the soul of everyone as the life of soul itself.

Facing in this direction to develop individual soul life—through giving attention to dreams, imaginatively picturing myths, and going into our pathologies with imagination instead of trying to stamp them out—relativizes the ego. But it cannot result in a capacity to experience the I more substantially, as the I can be experienced only in relation with the outer world. Relativizing the ego can be a help here, however; for the I also cannot be experienced as long as ego is at the center.

Austrian philosopher-clairvoyant Rudolf Steiner first set me on a course of imagining the I as an aspect of the soul's participation in the future.[1] The work of Jung, revisioned through the archetypal psychology of James Hillman and Thomas Moore and brought into a synthesis with Steiner, can begin to open a vision, not from the past, but from the future.

Steiner's understanding of the relation between soul and ego is based on his understanding of the relation of soul and time.[2] There is, few would argue, a current of time running from the past into the present toward the future. The soul lives in part in this current of time, expressing itself through images of past events and concepts we have learned in the past. These images and concepts, which would also include the realm of archetypal images, do not express themselves directly in consciousness. In fact, Steiner astutely observes, consciousness cannot even be accounted for on the basis of this time current alone.

Steiner then draws attention to another current of time, something not normally observed but actually quite obvious. We need pay only the slightest attention to daily life to notice that we meet the world not only from what lives from the past, but also from an intuition of what is coming. Words which are commonly associated with soul—words such as longing, desire, hope, anxiety, anticipation, need, want, and even despair, all have a strong reference to the future. Suddenly, we realize that soul has an intense interest in the future.

So there is a second current of time, a real and substantial current that comes to us from the future, flows into the present, and toward the past! The place where the current from the past and the current from the future overlap is in the human body, and the region of overlap is the domain of consciousness.

Further, this consciousness cannot be equated with ego consciousness. We are conscious while awake, but only from time to time are we aware in consciousness of the quality of "I" consciousness. So, the I is an additional factor, a third factor not accounted for by the current of time from the past or the one from the future, or by their overlap. What, then, accounts for the experience of I?

A quite amazing aspect of the experience of ourselves as an I is that such an experience is not learned. The elaboration of the experience is learned, so who I picture myself to be has a great deal to do with how this I was treated by others—whether loved or despised, cherished or abused. The experience is also greatly influenced by the archetypal images of the individual soul. But the I experience itself emerges quite spontaneously in human development, at about the age of three. It is as if the I, a unifying and synthesizing factor in consciousness, is quite suddenly inserted into the living stream of human time. Its presence makes each individual aware of a separation between the inner and outer streams of time, and changes the sense of time to one occurring from moment to moment rather than as a continuous duration.

Animals, Steiner says, do not have this kind of consciousness and so live in a complete continuity of inner and outer time; when an outer event has passed, it does not linger on as a conscious memory for the animal. On the other hand, each of us can be in a quite different time than the time of the outer world. Someone may be talking to me in the present moment, for example, while I am at the same moment experiencing a vivid image from the past or already picturing a future.

Once present, this experience of ourselves as an I is nonetheless greatly influenced by the time current from the past—so much so that we all think that who we are has to do with what affects us from the past. The original unity of the I with the time currents from the future and the past is quickly reduced to the ego and the time current from the past. Nearly the whole of therapeutic psychology is based on this sense of being affected by the past. This continues in spite of the fact that everyone, without exception, enters therapy in order to find a way into the future, a way back to the I and a view of the world as coming to be.

True, much of the inability to move into the future is due to blocks from the past. Equally so, however, we remain completely ignorant of how to live more out of the time current from the future than out of that from the past. It is as if half of psychology has been completely ignored. The soul's connection with the time current from the future, with what is coming to be rather than what has already been—this is the soul's connection, through the I, with the Soul of the World.

The event of the bomb, in scrambling the time current from the past, is at the same time destroying the sense of the ego as based on what has been given from the past. A new sense of ego is now demanded: one capable of imagining who we can be rather than acting out of what has influenced us from the past. Here, we suddenly begin to perceive dimly how achieving independence from the past makes possible the development of new capacities.

An entirely new consciousness awaits, though it is not easily entered. First, it is to be noted that what we usually imagine as the future is nothing more than a projection of the past into a future time, elaborated through fantasy. Science fiction always works with this kind of projection. In truth, the future is the current of the not-already-known. The work, then, concerns the development of capacities to live in the not-already-known, fully consciously.

Precedents do exist for living in the time that is not-known. Anyone in love lives in this time current from the future. While one is in love, the past is forgotten; one forgets the inbuilt limitations stemming from the past. All seems possible, and one sees only the future because it is right before one's eyes. The gift of love is the truth, not only the truth of seeing an other human being, but the truth of the world. But once given as a gift, this offering withdraws, and what was given as feeling must then be earned by accomplishing the same kind of perception through hard work. Few accomplish the deed.

Through the activity of love, we learn of our own darkness as well as that of the beloved. But the great secret of love is that continuing to love in the face of such darkness is not contingent on overcoming what is despised in ourselves and the other; it depends on entering ever more fully into this element with the force of love, which produces an alchemical transmutation of both. This precedent of living in the time current from the future indicates that living in relation with the Soul of the World requires coming to see the substance of the I as love. But this has to be an entirely new sense of love, because the most significant loss accompanying the destruction of living from the time current from the past is the breakdown of love as it has been given to us from tradition. To be able to work consciously toward this new kind of love, we must first characterize the complex character of love in relation to the world.

Love in the World

Love entered the human world with the separation of the sexes and took the form of sexual desire. The separation of the sexes is told as a myth in Plato's *Symposium,* a story with which we are all familiar. Sexual desire can be described as the love of the body for the body. The body is attracted to other bodies, as if desiring something needed to complete itself. This kind of love has a strong impersonal component, an instinctual character, an aspect of the Soul of the World that calls for completeness in the human being just as there is completeness in the world.

As a human instinct, however, this kind of love is different from all other instincts. If we do not eat or drink we will die; but if we do not have sex, death will not result. Thus, with this instinct there is an element of freedom, albeit a quite minimal element. This element of freedom makes it possible not only to receive pleasure through the body, but also to give pleasure. Further, this strong bodily nature of love assures that love will not abandon the physical realm.

Concurrent with sexual desire, for a long time love manifested as a force in the blood. In times past one did not marry a stranger, but someone with whom there was a connection of the blood, someone of the same clan, tribe, or family. The modern family is a remembrance of this kind of love, the strong ties of the blood. And family life is still generally characterized by the fact that it is easier to love one's own flesh and blood than a stranger. In our time, it is also easier to kill a family member than a stranger, and it is certainly easier to abuse one. These pathologies, now rampant, indicate that the time of love through the blood is past.

If a type of love that was appropriate at a given time continues after that time, violence comes to predominate over love. This fact does not mean that family life is at an end, though it is being and will have to be further revisioned, to the point that family life will no longer be based on the pattern of blood love. The time of love through the blood actually ended long ago, but the form of this love was transferred to the soul. Thus, as Freud saw so clearly, we unconsciously look for someone to father or mother us, and call this love. When this kind of attraction occurs, it now leads to disastrous relationships.

Besides sexual love, love through blood relationships, and blood love transferred to the realm of the soul, there is also the attraction of one person to another. In addition to love of the body for the body, there is love for this body and not that body, something more personal. This kind of attraction is emotional love, indicating that there is something to be worked out between two souls; a karmic element of unfinished work to do brings people together in a personal way. Often, however, the emotional attraction does not in itself indicate the nature of this work, which may be trying and terribly hard work, full of conflict. When people who come together for this reason begin to feel the true character of the work, they often separate. Also, in many instances, when the work to be done between two souls has been completed, then there seems no longer to be an emotional bond.

There are still other kinds of love. There is self-love, love turned toward oneself, the source of selfishness. Then, there is a further kind of love—love for a particular person who encompasses the core being of the person. This is true individual love, the love of an individual for an individual. Everyone who falls in love visualizes this as the true nature of the attraction, even though, most often, the intensity of the emotional pull confuses personal love with true individual love. Individual love is an intuition that we have from the time current from the future, but it is not something given in the way that desire or emotion is given; it will have to be created.

Love is so pervasive that no aspect of human existence can be found devoid of the quality of love. Distinguishing all these forms of love is certainly not easy in practice. At this point, however, our question concerns where all these kinds of love come from. What kind of consciousness is love that asserts itself in the body, blood, social life, emotional life, and individual life? This question cannot be answered without taking into central account the place of the enactment of loves of all types—the Earth.

Someone might want to argue for spiritual love and say that all love here is but a reflection of a higher love. The Russian philosopher, theologian, and mystic, Vladimir Soloviev in his masterful work, *The Meaning of Love,* answers such an argument thus:

> So-called spiritual love is a phenomenon which is not only abnormal, but also completely purposeless, because the separation of the spiritual from the sensuous to which such love aspires, is accomplished without it, and in the best possible way by death. True spiritual love is not a feeble imitation and anticipation of death, but a triumph over death, not a separation of the immortal from the mortal, of the eternal from the temporal, but a transfiguration of the mortal into the immortal, the acceptance of the temporal into the eternal. False spirituality is a denial of the flesh, true spirituality is the regeneration of the flesh, its salvation, its resurrection from the dead.[3]

Human beings are beings of love through and through. Why? Because human beings are Earth beings. The Earth, says Rudolf Steiner, is the cosmos of love. He means by this that Wisdom, the Soul of the World, is destined to become consciousness, and this takes place through Wisdom transformed into love. She has been working toward this transformation for a very long time—working through the body, then the blood, then the emotions, then through the self—and she has now started to work into individuality itself. The future of love concerns the full development of individuality, or of the I, which will then be responsible for the creation of a new, conscious unity of the world, brought forth out of the freedom of the I as love.

The forms of love from the past have been severely damaged as a result of the kind of consciousness responsible for the atomic bomb. None of these forms has the strength to hold together relationships without being renewed through the development of individual love. Individual love, on the other hand, cannot develop in isolation from the world because individual love is at the same time world-oriented love.

There is much talk these days about the living Earth. Mostly it is an idea, albeit a much better idea than the Earth as inanimate source of resources. This idea can be an actual experience. Will Brinton, who heads the Woods End Institute in Maine and has pioneered composting on a large scale (among the clients of Woods End is Disney World), once suggested an interesting exercise. When you walk on the Earth, imagine that this is the skin of a live being. Imagine the flow of waters in streams and rivers as the blood of this being. Imagine the air you breathe as her breath. This simple act will bring an uncanny experience which is hard to stay in for long. Once it is experienced, however, the source of love is more easily understood. For with this experience comes the question: Who are we? Are we parasites living off of this being like fleas on the back of a dog? Are we not of her substance? Is not, then, our consciousness an expression of her, and the development toward individuality an expression of the Wisdom of Earth transforming into love that is fully individual?

Imagine someone incapable of developing the force of love; we have a picture of someone whose inner being is dried up. Such a person is a distressing sight, for love is a living force that keeps the body alive. Without love we would actually perish, physically die. Fortunately, even the greatest egotist cannot completely empty his or her being of the force of love. If one is incapable of loving anything else, it is at least possible to love money.

But love cannot be generated by human beings alone. We are transformers and transmitters, elaborators, and even co-creators of this force, but not its creators. This Eternal Feminine being of Earth is its source. From this understanding, then, we can re-ask the question, "Who am I?"

I am Earth in her manifestation as consciousness. I am that quality of consciousness that is the quality of warmth, of feeling. I am not separate from thinking, for wherever there is warmth of thinking I am there. And I am not separate from willing and doing, for wherever there is the fire of will I am there. I have no content. I am pure activity.

As yet, the quality of warmth of consciousness, of feeling, is dreamlike. It occurs only momentarily and then seems to vanish. When not there, it is as if its presence were a dream; one has difficulty in trying to make the dream reappear or make the memory of it stay clear.

When the attraction of love between people exists, this quality tends to be more permanent. The difficulties in love and relationships have a great deal to do with the fact that the world is usually left out of the love. Love, however, does not occur just between two people. It springs up in the context of the world, in this place of Earth. If we try to keep it for ourselves and do not return it enlarged to the world and thus to Earth, it either vanishes or seems to turn into conflict and separation. Love itself does not actually turn sour; rather, its opposite, destruction comes to the fore to balance the damming up of this force.

Love must circulate in order to get out of its dreamy state. When it does not circulate, it becomes sought after in desperation, as if it were rare and difficult to find. Love is rare only when it hides, and it hides when it is taken up for our own use and not returned.

Vaclav Havel, the former president of the former Czechoslovakia, is a contemporary instance of one who speaks out of this new kind of imagining, the ego filled with the activity of love. In a speech made to the World Economic Forum in Davos, Switzerland on February 4, 1991, he stated:

> It is my profound conviction that we have to release from the sphere of private whim such forces as: a natural, unique and unrepeatable experience of the world, an elementary sense of justice, the ability to see things as others do, a sense of transcendental responsibility, archetypal wisdom, good taste, courage, compassion, and faith in the importance of particular measures that do not aspire to be a universal key to salvation. . . . Soul, individual spirituality, firsthand personal insight into things; the courage to be himself and go the way his conscience points, humility in the face of the mysterious order of Being, confidence in its natural direction and, above all, trust in his own subjectivity as his principal link with the subjectivity of the world—these are qualities that politicians of the future should have.[4]

This is Sophianic language! Having "unique and unrepeatable experience of the world" means that past content is not relied upon. One must create, create, create, without end. Archetypal wisdom is the realm of Sophia, the very meaning of her name. Having a sense of the importance of particulars indicates that the time of system and abstraction is at an end. The fall of communism, says Havel, cannot be seen as simply the end of a political regime. It is the end, the crisis, of modern thought—thinking with thoughts that have already been thought, attempting to explain and control everything that exists, the mentality of exploitation. Then, the chief indicator that here we have someone who speaks out of the impulse of Sophia is the reliance on one's own subjectivity—one's own sense of I, which is the link with the subjectivity of the world. Earth is not an it, but a thou.

One might well look at this speech and feel that here we have a formula for failure, for Havel was not able to keep his country from fragmenting. What value is truth if it does not result in success? However, we are just at the very beginning of a new process, a process that will unfold gradually over the next centuries. We need instances of those who see and stand for what they see. What Havel sees must be seen by many individuals in completely individual ways, for he is not prescribing a new system. To work in this way, toward this new vision, is to work not for ourselves but for the future of the Earth.

Re-membering the Body and the World

Marshall McLuhan, that great forgotten sage, brilliantly described how a fragmentation of the body has come about through a technologizing of the world. All technology is a matter of extending aspects of the body into the world. Walking, for example, is extended into the world with the invention of the wheel. Not only is the capacity of the body to move incorporated into an object, it is also accelerated. The body cannot cope with this acceleration, and thus becomes numb. When I walk, the world is perceived as "all around." When I ride a bicycle, I feel more like I am going through the world. When I ride in a car, the world begins to get flat and goes by as if in front of an observer. When I fly, the world disappears, and so does the body. Thus, after flying, it takes time to recover the sense of the body.

McLuhan speaks of this numbing effect of acceleration as an "autoamputation" of the senses. With the computer, thinking is externalized and accelerated, and the brain is autoamputated. With the bomb, the body as a sensing, experiencing, feeling, living totality has been autoamputated; this is an effect of fear spread throughout the world as a result of the power of destructiveness over all of life.

The living body of the Earth cannot be re-membered unless we re-member our own bodies, a primary act of love. The numbing of the body needs to be recognized and re-enlivening must occur. We are losing the body and rapidly becoming automatons that look like human beings from the outside, but are hollow inside.

By enlivening I do not refer here to bodywork, to massage, acupuncture, ritual, hot baths, Rolfing, recovery work, or any of the rest, for these methods, as effective as they might be, leave out the body of the world. The thought that if we first enliven our own bodies then we can go on and enliven the body of Earth is false because it operates out of a dualism. The individual benefits of these ways of recovering body are undeniable, but noble and even idealistic egotisms cannot alone be effective for what is needed to balance the bomb. For this work, re-membering the body requires at the same time re-membering the world; the two cannot be separated. Further, since we are trying to speak out of a sense of the time current from the future that is coming toward us, this remembering cannot be of the past, trying to recollect something that has been left behind. We are now required to begin learning how to remember the world as it comes to be present to the body every moment.

First, some things concerning memory. Memory is a magical act in which things not present are evoked. Memory of things past reproduces an impression from the past, but this reproducing is at the same time an imagining; that is to say, it is more than an imprint and more than a copy. Thus, for example, if there is a circle of people and the first person tells a story, and then the second one tells it again according to memory, then the third, and so on, by the time the story returns to the beginning of the circle, it will be very different due to the element of imagination in memory. Imagination is the active, creating element of memory which goes beyond the past.

Further, several types of memory need to be distinguished. There is mechanical memory, in which remembrance simply happens but is based on association. Thus, if I see something, say a woman wearing a broad-brimmed yellow hat, a host of associations from the past may surface—my aunt wearing a funny yellow hat, the hat given to me for Christmas when I was small, the hat my wife wore last Easter. Then, there is logical memory, in which it is necessary to think in order to remember things. In trying to remember all of these kinds of memory, for example, I may remember two, but also remember that there are more. I then have to actively search for the rest.

A third kind of memory could be called moral memory, which has to do not with morality or moralism, but rather with the degree of interest one has in the world. Moral memory is a matter of the heart. When the heart is involved, things will be remembered which fail automatic or logical memory. Can anyone forget their first love?

A fourth kind of memory is memory in a vertical direction. This memory is not memory in the horizontal direction, the evocation of things past, but memory of things eternal. The actual experience of soul or of spirit, for example, cannot occur through persuasion that such realities exist. The felt sense of soul or of spirit is a memory coming from above and below. It is not possible to account for these experiences based on the past.

The kind of memory I want now to introduce relies on memory in the vertical direction and on moral memory, the memory of the heart. With the above descriptions concerning what memory does and the several ways it operates, we can begin to sense that the act of recollection holds the body together as a unified whole. We get closer to what memory is, its true function and magic.

Without memory, the body sense is fragmented into parts. Memory constitutes the activity through which the body stays close to itself as a whole being. Memorizing, for example, is an act through which something that is foreign and alien is folded back into oneself and becomes oneself; that which existed apart and alone is folded into the totality of the body. Through memory we become aware of ourselves as embodied in a continuous way.

With the advent of the kind of consciousness that brought about the atomic bomb, however, nothing is left to re-member. All memory of the past becomes more or less a sham, trying to hold on to something that can no longer be put back together in the same way.

Memory must now take a new form, the form of a creating activity that occurs in the present, an active work of remembering the body in every ongoing perception of the world. That is to say, memory now becomes a mode of knowing the world. With the loss of the sense of the body as unified, we look out at the world as if from a tiny peephole through the barrier of the armored body. We walk through the world as if inside a military tank. From such a perspective, the world does not seem to be continuous with ourselves, but rather something "over there" in the distance, which we view with an onlooker consciousness that is detached and removed.

As I write these thoughts, I look out of my window and see a stand of trees—over there. There are pine trees and birch trees, dense and thick in the darkness of a clouded sky. For a moment, it is possible to feel that what is "over there" is at the same time right here where my body is. I, so to speak, fold back what is over there into the space of my own body, an act of remembering the present. This kind of activity is needed, for the past no longer carries us into the present in a living way, in a way that makes us feel naturally that we belong to the world. The world is now alien, other, hidden, and must be approached in acts of conscious love. In this small act of remembering the world, there is also a remembering of the presence of the body. Knowing the world through active remembering of the present is at the same time a way of knowing oneself—remembering the world by recalling oneself back to oneself.

One may be quite willing, and even interested in seeking to know the world through active remembering of the body, given the kind of example just pictured. But consider another instance: I am walking down a street in Greenwich Village in New York City. It is nine o'clock on an early spring evening, one of the first warm evenings. As I walk, the streets are filled with people, and there on a street corner I see a man selling drugs to a teenager. I feel nausea, and also fear, for this is one rough dude. I feel anger that the teen is so naive—there is an impulse to judge it all. But instead, I try to take what is happening back into my body, to feel how what is over there is also right here. The act of memory here takes me into grief.

Attentiveness to such small acts of perception begins to reveal that nothing in the world need be foreign, that all of the world is also us, and that knowing the world in this way is also a discipline of self-knowledge, of knowing oneself. In intellectual knowing, we know about things. In memory, we know ourselves in knowing the world. All such knowing is painful, memory as mourning, as a wounding. The painfulness of memory is felt in the region of the heart, knowing as feeling, and feeling awakening from its dream-like state.

Further, with this kind of knowing a longing mixed with sorrow is awakened; it is simply there, spontaneous with body feeling, and quite surprising. This longing and sorrow do not seem to be related to the particular nature of the perception, for they are present whether in the presence of the woods or of the drug transaction. Quite mysterious, but revealing, is the realization that to work at this new way of knowing requires a kind of courage—not heroic, but simply the capacity to stay with what presents itself. This aspect of memory will be explored further in the following chapter; just as I have only begun to touch on love, so also am I here describing only the first moment of the act of re-membering the unity of the body in relation to the unity of the world.

What could be the source of the longing and sorrow that come with attempting to remember the world? I believe these deep feelings have to do with what is lost in learning to know through the realm of the heart. While the modern world is finished we still live in the habits of that worldview, which are inscribed in every cell of every body. Havel, in his speech to the World Economics Forum, gives a picture of this worldview that helps us understand that when we try to recover the body of the world, we feel also the longing and sorrow that come with relinquishing a habit, an addiction:

> The modern era has been dominated by the culminating belief, expressed in different forms, that the world—and Being as such—is a wholly knowable system governed by a finite number of universal laws that man can grasp and rationally direct for his own benefit. This era, beginning in the Renaissance and developing from the Enlightenment to Socialism, from positivism to scientism, from the industrial revolution to the information revolution, was characterized by rapid advance in rational, cognitive thinking.
>
> This, in turn, gave rise to the proud belief that man, as the pinnacle of everything that exists, was capable of objectively describing, explaining and controlling everything that exists, and of possessing the one and only truth about the world. It was an era in which there was a cult of depersonalized objectivity, and era in which objective knowledge was amassed and technically exploited, an era of belief in automatic progress brokered by the scientific method.[5]

In small acts of knowing through the heart, knowing through subjectivizing what is given, making all knowing personal and heartfelt, the habit of the modern world is broken; and it has to be broken over and over again. Just as an alcoholic is always an alcoholic, we also live on in the habit of the modern world, even though it is dead. The longing and sorrow of really perceiving the body of the world is, at least in part, an act of mourning and grieving for the loss of this dominating worldview. If the loss of this habit is not grieved, it will return and assert itself like a ghost.

When I look out my window at the trees and simultaneously feel the trees here where my body is as well as there in the world, it begins to become apparent that the system of ecological management of the environment will never take care of the world for me. I feel sorrow that I cannot rely on this modern illusion, and I long for the lost illusion. When I see the drug dealer selling death to the teen, and I feel that is happening here where my body is as well as there in the world, it begins to dawn on me that the system of drug laws, drug treatment, and drug education will never take care of the drug problem. I feel sorrow that the illusion of an objective system will not work, and I long for the false idea that some mechanism, some ideology, some doctrine will take care of things.

The end of the modern world is not the end of science and not the end of technology. The thought that this might be the case would be an attempt to go back to the far past, which is in any case gone. The end of the modern world, with respect to science and technology, means that these activities take their place in the totality rather than attempting to govern and at the same time define the world by creating a theory of what is right before our eyes.

The time current from the future, as I have pointed out, is the realm of the not-known. Through the event and imagination of the bomb we now live in this current of time. Here is where love becomes a possibility as a new way of knowing, a knowing of the heart. Here is where the I comes into its own as the activity of fully conscious imagining. Its first act concerns remembering the body of the world through remembering the world within us. Now, it is time to ask how this way of proceeding can be sustained.

What makes possible going on when one is lost? Love is a part of the answer, but there is another part as well. Going on in the realm of the unknown is a question of will. Heroic will, will that comes from the capacities of the past informing an ego that can do something in the world—that sense of will no longer has the needed power. It simply does not work—not in politics, not in marriage, not in education, not in economics, nowhere. The quality of will that, combined with the growing capacity to know through the heart, enables us to move on in the realm of the unknown is reverence. This religious, pious-sounding word is worthy of exploration.

In the region of the not-known, it is entirely possible to lose oneself by letting go and fainting into the undefined darkness. Impotence results. Will is lost. Further, if the sense of the I working now through the activity of love is not also maintained through the activity of imaginative thinking, then love becomes sentimentalism. The path I am trying to describe, the Grail path of soul and spirit in the world, not spirit above and soul below, raises the question of how to remain conscious. The answer is love of the unknown and a constant vigilance of inner activity. These two activities together describe reverence.

The sentimental ego, wandering through life as if asleep, and the ego unwilling to be aware of itself are in very great danger of being taken over by something or someone that offers the promise of love and the promise of knowing how to do it. This danger takes many forms, including cults, various psychotherapies, hypnotherapies, reprogramming, dogmatism and fanaticism in religions. Anything that would dim, confuse, bypass, or try to eliminate the sense of the I retards the necessary activity of finding the way into the future.

5

GRIEVING, LOVE,
AND THE SOUL

As we explored briefly in chapter 3, the life of the individual body and the life of Earth are inseparably bound to each other through a common membrane. This membrane is known variously in esoteric literature as the subtle body, or etheric body, the *pranamayakosa* of Yoga and Tibetan Buddhism, and by many other names. It is the point of focus in Chinese acupuncture and in martial arts such as kung fu. The "Pistis Sophia" story of the creation through Sophia describes the subtle body in terms of the forming qualities of the elements of earth, water, air, and fire.

Let us recall that the elements are rhythmical activity which compose the body of Earth as a living being and also the human body as living. They are not substances but forming activities which bring about unity of living form. For example, every seven years the physical substance of the body is completely replaced with new substance; the body still retains its form as an individual human body during this constant metamorphosis, however, due to the activity of elemental etheric forces interweaving the physical body. These etheric forces are not mechanical in nature. As we saw in the story of the creating of the body of Earth, the condensing of the elements through these forces is at the same time the activity of the living being of Sophia.

The replacement of the substance of the body in a seven-year rhythm is not due simply to the wearing out of this substance over time. We must ask what is responsible for ageing, or dying. As far as the substance of the physical body is concerned, this process is accelerated by radioactivity. Radioactivity is first of all a world process that is not confined to special mineral substances. The minerals containing uranium, thorium, and the like are not alone responsible for radioactivity; all earth substances contain, to a degree, this death-making element. Radioactive substance is also mingled with the air and with the oceans, rain, and snow. In the Sophia story, the counter-creation of Earth by the lion-faced being filled with pride is an image of this death-dealing element of radioactivity that permeates everything just as the creating activity permeates everything.

The first step toward the discovery of radiation occurred in 1895 when an assistant of Roentgen, the researcher into x-rays, laid down, by chance, a bunch of keys on top of an unopened box of photographic plates near a cathode ray tube. When the plates were developed, an eerie image of the keys, left as if by a ghost, showed forth. This accidental discovery of radiation inspired Becquerel to investigate the florescence of minerals placed in the cathode ray tube, through which he discovered certain uranium compounds. Based on these experiments, the Curies were able to isolate the element of radium, which was found to be continuously disintegrating. Madame Curie died a painful death of leukemia as a result of her experiments with radioactivity, an indication of the forces involved.

Radiation has entered the present world, not just as a deadly force accompanying atomic explosions, but as something that appears useful and helpful for everyday life. Vegetables are radiated to prevent spoiling, and meat is similarly treated; the medical profession uses various kinds of radiation, not only in x-rays, but in other diagnostic and treatment modalities. Nuclear energy plants are widespread, but the far-reaching effects of such plants are unknown, except when they melt down; already many factories which produced radioactive materials for industry and weapons, such as Rocky Flats in suburban Denver, Colorado, are completely contaminated.

In addition, the program for developing atomic weapons is far from over, for a large number of underground explosions are planned. Add to this the fact that other nations such as North Korea, France, and China are continuing to develop nuclear programs. Besides nuclear radiation, there are also all the effects of electromagnetic radiation—from high-power electric lines, microwaves, communication satellites, television and computer screens, and cellular phones. These kinds of radiation have the same effect on the etheric body as atomic radiation does. Thus, it becomes clear that it is not possible to escape. The physicist Ernst Lehrs, described the effect of all this radiation:

> With every act of setting electromagnetic energies in motion we interfere with the entire levity-gravity balance of our planet by turning part of the Earth's coherent substance into cosmic "dust." Thus we may say that whenever we generate electricity we speed up the Earth's process of cosmic ageing. Obviously this is tremendously enhanced by the creation of artificial radioactivity.[1]

Radiation is ghostlike, piercing through the living body of the world and the human body, accelerating the process of ageing and dying. This emissary of death withers the life force of every earthly being. Radiation, however, often kills slowly, working not directly on the physical body, but on the subtle body. It can be monitored through devices which measure its effects, and "acceptable" levels have been determined. But such measurements can determine only at what level this force becomes damaging to the physical body. Since the etheric body is not even recognized as a reality by standard science, "acceptable" levels of radiation may well be damaging the life force over a long period of time, even over generations.

Radioactivity is most strongly marked in substances having the greatest atomic weight, and the products of radioactive dissolution are isotopes of lead. Thus, dissolution of living body substance due to radioactivity is similar to substances turning into lead. In times when such things were seen without the aid of scientific apparatus, this state of dissolution was always accompanied by the sign of Saturn. Depression, heaviness, literalness, concern with death, illness, disease, darkness, are all Saturn qualities. When the natural balance between the creating activities of the elements and the dissolving qualities of radioactivity is interfered with such that dissolution begins to predominate, we can expect an increase in the expression of the qualities of Saturn in the world.

At the same time, dissolution has another side. The alchemists began their work, in fact, with a process of dissolution; Saturn is at the beginning of alchemical transformation. Thus, they understood that going through Saturn can lead to regeneration. I want to show a parallel in the modern world: The disruption of the subtle body of the Earth and of the human body in the direction of dissolution, if met and faced, can lead to a regenerating force through which soul begins to be conscious as the I.

Grieving as the Activation of Conscious Soul Life

When the dissolving action of radioactivity attacks simultaneously the subtle body of the Earth and the human etheric activity, we experience not only depression or concern for death, disease, or illness, but also grieving. The Chernobyl disaster gives a condensed picture of the attack on the etheric body released by the force of radiation in the world. Years after it, many people still live in the region. The landscape is desolate, not unlike what a landscape would look like after an atomic explosion. The people have to grow and eat potatoes in soil contaminated by radiation. Their animals have tumors; nevertheless, these animals must serve as food. The people also have extremely high rates of cancer. When we see this tragedy, a deep sense of grieving springs forth. We grieve for those people, for the land, and for the sickness of life. But the grief is yet deeper, for this scene tells us that life as it once was is no longer possible. What those people experience in an intense way images the condition and situation of Earth as a whole.

Grief is a wholly bodily experience. It is more than sympathy, and more than compassion. While we may look at a scene from Chernobyl for but a few moments, the shock of seeing it draws us into their grieving, for their grieving is also ours. If we let go of the anger and the denial for only a moment, the full feeling is experienced, deeper even than that accompanying the loss of a loved one, for this event of radiation in the world signals the loss of what life has been. Every cell of the body feels this loss, and within each one of us exists a deep and uncontrollable sobbing which has not, for most, come to the surface as yet. When a loved one dies, grieving never ceases; it becomes a permanent aspect of life, but at the same time it can be the activation of a conscious soul life.

Grieving has become more open and recognized in the past several years. The men's movement engages in rituals that bring about grieving. People in recovery from abuse go through grieving for the love they never received. People who have suffered trauma such as rape or have been the victims of crime, similarly go through grieving in order to be able to face the world again.

I believe that the prevalence of this emotion is something more than personal, something more than a psychological process belonging to individuals. Grieving is world-oriented, and those who have entered into this deep emotion are expressing what we all feel and are afraid to face. The activation of an active, conscious soul life in the face of the present world is necessary and unavoidable. We see grieving all around us, for this condition is us. Our Earth, this source of love, is dying; no measurements of science can tell us otherwise; no continued cover-ups by government, by industry, by the military, can hide what is felt in the immediacy of the soul experience of the body. As long as this is denied, what belongs to the world will continue to be interpreted as only personal psychological suffering, when in fact it is at the same time a world-suffering.

Activation of soul consciousness through grieving brings soul into conjunction with the ego, initiating a new sense of the I. It develops an I that is no longer so concerned with self-preservation, self-isolation, and self-achievement, but is oriented instead toward recreating the world through the activity of imagination given force through love. Where ego was, this I seems to say, there imagining shall be.

The ego cannot work toward such a task out of its own powers, powers gained through all that was given from a past now unavailable as natural and living. Instead, we now must be open to the current of time from the future. We need to learn to live in this current of possibility, which can be formed into the weaving of picture-making, now fully conscious. What formerly occurred unconsciously, the imaginal activity of soul life, must now begin to take place consciously. This new task is like someone who has been given a large inheritance, only to wake up one morning to find that the market has crashed; a person in such a situation would most likely go through grieving, and out of this grieving learn how to set out to accomplish oneself what was before taken for granted. In the realm of the imaginal I, such a work begins with learning to be conscious of the body in soul, developing an imagination of the activity of the body. Let us explore some indications of how this can be done, and then go on to see how love is central to such a task.

Getting in Touch with the World

Grieving is a process through which the body gradually becomes a conscious body in soul. It is as if, in grieving, every cell of the body becomes conscious and it begins to be possible to sense the world through the body as a whole. Such a mode of sensing is quite different than that of experiencing the world by way of the individual senses, for sensing through the body as a whole is at the same time sensing the world as a whole.

One might think that this amounts to blooming, buzzing confusion; but, in fact, it is a presence to particularities in their essence. For example, someone who goes through a time of grieving over the loss of a loved one is in great pain. At the same time, this individual has a heightened sense of what is essential and what is not essential. Such a person has a difficult time relating with others, not because of depression, but because it is readily apparent that most people do not live with this sense of the essential, and much that goes on around the grieving person is seen as trivial. The perception, I think, is true. When the pain of grieving eases, often the capacity to sense the essential does not go away with it. I am not suggesting that the way to wholeness is through being in constant pain, but by recognizing that pain signals the loss of an old ego sense and can signal the birth of a new, conscious sensibility in relation to the world and others.

The organ for sensing the world as a synthesis of the whole, for sensing particularities and yet at the same time sensing that everything is indeed related to everything else, is the skin. Through the organ of the skin, the body mirrors what is around it. Imagine a father walking down the street with his three-year-old son. The boy jumps in a puddle of muddy water. The father shouts, "Stop that! You know better than to get all wet and muddy!" The three-year-old child cannot cognitively understand what his father is saying, but his body mirrors the mood, the voice, the gesture of his father—and does so everywhere in the body—by a tightening, a freezing, a contraction. This mirroring goes on all the time, not just in childhood.

Mirroring happens with all of us all of the time. We are not usually aware of it unless in the presence of anger or shouting, or in the presence of warm and caring gestures and actions. Further, the body mirrors everything in its surroundings, even things which are not visible, such as the emotional state of others, even if emotion is not being expressed.

A better, more descriptive word than mirroring is _touch_. The body experiences the surrounding world as a whole through a sensing that is like touch, but this sensing through touch does not necessarily involve being physically touched. The body knows its surroundings through touch, which also occurs from a distance—in principle, any distance. While the skin is the organ for experiencing the touch of the world, it does not have to be in physical contact with what touches it any more than the eye has to be in physical contact with an object in order to see it. Through practicing attentiveness to the body, the sense of touch can become a conscious way of experiencing the world, not as a world of objects, but as a world of activity.

To sense in this way, we have to rid ourselves of the concept of the body as an object and begin to feel the body as activity, as an image in process that we are within. The living, human body is not an object in the same way a chair or a lamp is an object. The argument can of course be made that if I step out into the street and get hit by a car, that is definite verification that my body is an object like other objects. To be able to say that one aspect of the human body is an object-quality, however, does not verify that all of it is an object; the body is that and much more, and the much more is not added on like extra accessories.

Only when the body is touched as an object is touched does it become an object among other objects. I can feel like I was just run over by an automobile when someone mistreats me. I can also feel like an object when the picture-weaving activity of the etheric body weakens.

Conscious attentiveness to the life of the body as felt within oneself does not mean being aware of one's own body as an onlooker. It means beginning to sense the body as activity—not as an object that has properties of mobility, but as an imagining within mobility itself, as if, in waking life, the world is dreaming the body. The skin is the sense organ for experiencing this activity, and like all of the other sense organs it is more than a physiological receptor. The eye, for example, can be viewed as a complex physiological mechanism, but it is also a capacity, the capacity to see. All of the sense organs of the body are also capacities.

A sense organ is the body's evolutionary response to a wounding of the body. For example, fish that live in complete darkness in water within caves, and are no longer wounded by light, not only lose vision, but over generations the organ of the eye itself disappears. The skin is thus becoming a capacity through the fact that it is now wounded by the presence of radiation. It is a far more subtle organ than the other organs of the body, for it is the organ that opens the possibility of a psychic, soul presence to the world. The formation of this capacity of psychic awareness must, however, be in close connection with a soulful sense of I. Without the accompanying awareness of the I, the forming of this psychic sense of the body moves into one of two kinds of pathologies—armoring or dependence.

Wilhelm Reich discovered the pathological process of body armoring, and he did so precisely through the kind of thinking we have been engaged in here. That is, he was able to picture the body in its union with soul and spirit, and also to picture the body in its psychic functioning. Armoring is a rigidifying of the body due to trauma and fear. Echoing what we have been describing, Reich states:

> Because armored man is rigidified, he thinks predominantly in terms of matter. He perceives motion as being in the beyond or as supernatural. This must be taken literally. Language always expresses the immediate condition of organ sensations and offers

an excellent clue to man's self awareness. Movement, i.e., plasmatic current, is indeed inaccessible to the rigidified human animal. It is therefore "beyond," i.e., beyond his ego perceptions; or "supernatural," i.e., felt as an eternal cosmic longing beyond his material being. What the armored organism perceives as "mind" or "soul" is the motility that is closed to him. . . . There it is, this motility; it lives, laughs, cries, hates, loves—but always only in a mirror. In reality it is barred to the ego, as the fruits were out of reach for Tantalus. From this tragic situation springs every murderous impulse, directed against life.[2]

Reich provided scientific evidence for the etheric body, showed that armoring was related to the formation of cancer, discovered the presence of the etheric body of the Earth, and showed the devastating effect of radiation on the etheric body of the Earth and that of human beings. He was also imprisoned by the U.S. government, ostensibly for transporting his device for strengthening the etheric body, the orgon box, across state lines. He died, reportedly of heart failure, a short time after being sent to prison.

Consciously working toward a body attentiveness, an attentiveness of the body as motility, strengthens the etheric body, the body in soul. We have to become our own "orgon" generators, able to be transported across state lines without fear of incarceration. In order to do so, however, we must keep in consciousness the vulnerability of the body to subtle forces. Armoring occurs only when the I is sleepy, unconscious, without a soul sense; then, in effect, the body can be hardened and the I imprisoned, as if inside a closed cavern.

The current epidemic phenomenon of codependency provides another picture of body armoring. The body that is armored longs for the experience of touch, which cannot be had because the body has become hardened due to trauma and fear. In the absence of the capacity to feel one's own body as activity, harmful touch—in the forms of physical abuse, sexual abuse, emotional abuse, all kinds of abuse—both increases armoring and, in a confused way, seems to offer the way out of it. This confusion constitutes the phenomenon of codependency.

Through fear, one becomes, as it were, encased inside the body, screaming for liberation. An abuser offers the needed touch of release, though in a harmful way because the abuser does not touch the body in soul, but the body as if it were an object—either physically, emotionally, or psychically. Indeed, abuse simply means that the body is treated as an object rather than a visible activity of soul. The result for the person abused is further body armoring, and increased need for touch.

Current treatment of codependency seems to offer a dual way of breaking such dependency. It begins with the effort to remember the trauma to the body, which results in deep grieving. Then one learns to establish boundaries, a kind of "healthy" armoring. This step is usually coupled with a spiritual program, such as the Twelve Steps—a reliance on the "supernatural," however one chooses to define this realm. In other words, instead of being shut off from a living, bodily presence to the world by the control of others, one learns to be in control of this process.

I do not mean to be critical of this therapeutic process, for it is undoubtedly beneficial. At the same time, body armoring can now also be seen as part of a much wider condition—for both abuser and abused are seeking the necessary life experience of being in touch with the world.

Love and the Soul of the Body

I want now to look at how love can be an active presence of individuality in the world, a real force that has real effects. First, it is necessary to emphasize the importance of approaching all of this through imagination. Radiation, seen through the imaginative activity of soul that is conscious, is simply a process of the disintegration of the soul factor in the world, a process in which both the Earth and the individual body are on the way to inertness, leadenness.

All of the life of Earth can be pictured as the radiance of Sophia as love, a pouring forth of herself in a completely selfless manner. Radiation can be seen as the disintegration of love's radiance, an activity coming to its end prematurely. To balance the process of disintegration, the activity of love must be strengthened, a process which now must take place from our side.

If love is not to be merely a platitude without real power, we must carefully differentiate its various qualities and aspects. To do so, we must return to the act of grieving. Rather than seeking the way out of it, we need to imagine grieving in a way that lets us see what it may unfold into.

We have described grieving as an awakening of soul consciousness in the body. Another way of stating this is that grieving is the activity of the body in sorrow, the underworld Sophianic quality of body life and experience. To move against grieving may be to move against Sophia. It may be an attempt by the ego in the old sense to remain in control by holding on to outmoded, accustomed ways of working. The old sense of the ego concerns the desire to know things before they are experienced, so that the experience can then be shaped according to what is already known. The new, conscious I as soul knows only in the experience itself, and not beforehand. Here, the I suffers experience. Suffering experience means undergoing it; it does not mean practicing masochism. We must ask, what makes this possible?

A picture. Imagine being out in the mountains, at a clear blue lake, a perfectly calm lake. You see in the lake the reflection of the blue sky above and great rolling clouds. You see also the reflection of the mighty pine trees, of an eagle flying overhead, and also the reflection of yourself. Someone then throws a stone into the lake; the reflection becomes wavy, unstable, and dizzying. The reflection is disrupted in two directions simultaneously, vertically—the sky, clouds, bird, trees—and horizontally, one's own image. The disruption of our own image is like the suffering of trauma. What goes unrecognized, however, is that this suffering is at the same time a disruption in the vertical direction, a disruption in the capacity to sense the world in its unity as a living body.

If one sought to repair only the image of oneself—if, for example, one could somehow steady that small part of the water which reflects one's body while leaving the rest of the water in turbulence—it would be only a short time before the unsteadying of one's own image would commence again. The only way to prevent the reappearance of disruption would be to make some kind of solid barrier around the reflected image of oneself. To work at steadying both the horizontal and the vertical dimensions of the wavering image, however, requires something larger than putting up a protective barrier, for a barrier cannot be found that encompasses the whole universe.

Uncovering an experience of trauma results in uncovering an individual living with shame. What is usually meant by shame is the feeling I have if I do not allow myself to be touched in a harmful way; I am shamed by the other for refusing to be an object for them. However, the experience of shame is actually twofold. On the one hand there is this individual sense of being shamed, which is unhealthy. On the other hand is the experience of shame felt whenever one suffers an isolation from the whole matrix of connections to which one belongs. These two experiences of shame are not easy to distinguish.

Healing individual shame without recognizing the need to turn love toward the world, not just toward oneself, can also obscure the necessary work of restoring balance to the world. Shame is a most important indicator that the connecting matrix of love has been harmed. That is to say, when one individual suffers the shame of trauma, the whole universe feels shame, so that the shame one feels is not just personal and individual. The extreme need for love that a person who is shamed feels is at the same time the cry of the Earth for restoration of her life force of love. The way toward restoring the life force of love in the world now begins through healthy self-love.

Self-love, these days, is equated with learning to love oneself. This, however, usually consists of nothing more than treating oneself as an object—often something one has worked hard to get away from when treated in such a manner by others. To say "I love myself" or to practice doing so in multifarious ways—including affirmations, taking care of oneself, being conscious of what you want for yourself, making sure that at last you are the first one you take care of in a relationship—is not self-love, but egotism. In fact, the dynamic of loving oneself in this way is really no different from the dynamic of hating oneself. To say "I hate myself" is also a form of egotism, for it also is a way of looking at oneself from the outside. What has yet to be discovered is that individuals who have been taught to love themselves suffer from abuse as much as those who have been taught to hate themselves, for they also have been taught to look upon themselves as objects.

One must try not to be judgmental of a word such as *egotism*; I am not saying that it is wrong or bad or ugly. I am trying to describe a process as clearly as possible in order to unravel some of the confusion surrounding love. Self-love is a necessity; without it love would have no individuality, and it would not be possible to freely choose to love another.

Self-love is built into the very nature of human consciousness; it does not have to be learned. What has to be learned is how to remove all of the obstacles of egotism that obscure the immediacy of the experience of self-love, and as well, how to do nothing to interfere with the natural emergence of self-love. Self-love is the basis of true human freedom, the experience of the I. It is an activity without an object, an originating activity, and it makes possible a free decision to turn this activity toward others and toward the world. Self-love is not the experience of loving oneself but rather the experience of "I love."

Conversely, to try to learn to love oneself by looking at oneself from the outside is to remain forever captivated. Self-love is difficult for those whose only experience of themselves is from the outside, and who believe others who tell them that they are good when they act one way and bad when they act another way.

Loving another is also often unrecognized self-love. When a person in love feels that he or she cannot live without the other, when love is accompanied by a swinging back and forth between all sorts of moods, then the other person is carrying an aspect of one's own soul, the aspect of self-love. This tragic situation is more or less the norm, because there is an expectation that love does not go together with the conscious sense of the I. One looks toward love as a way to be free from oneself. This kind of confusion concerning what love is about stems from an ego that is self-enclosed and separated from the world. Love seems to be a way back into the world, when, in fact, this kind of love does not release one from the self-enclosed ego, but takes one into the horrors of this enclosure, now found in the other person.

If I let someone else carry an aspect of my own soul, one which needs to be a conscious activity of my soulful I, a paralyzing fear emerges. If the other person leaves or threatens to leave, then I have a deep sense of abandonment. This abandonment in fact signifies that I am left without the element of self-love, which did not belong with the other person in the first place. Fear of this loss occasions all sorts of fantasies—the other person may leave; he or she is having an affair; I cannot let the other person out of sight; there is unbearable pain when the other person is not around. So I try to guarantee the presence of the other person through fear— threats of violence or actual violence, followed with deep sorrow and an intimacy that is too close. Then, when the other person acts in a way that does not conform to the missing part of oneself, this person is turned against with rage and hate.

Much love frequently springs only from poverty of soul consciousness. If we maintain that we could not live without the other one, then our own personality is impoverished, and we are seeking something that fulfills us. The whole thing, however, is veiled by saying: I love the other person.

What, then, is the nature of self-love if it is not the same as the affirmation "I love myself"? It is not a consciousness of oneself from the outside, looking, as it were, at oneself and affirming what one sees as good and worthy. Rather, self-love is equivalent to self-consciousness, and self-consciousness is not a consciousness of the self but a consciousness in the self.

Clarifying the true meaning of self-love helps to bring understanding to the relation between the ego and the I. Ego and I in fact refer to the same quality, the quality of self-consciousness, which can function in two directions; the I gives and the ego takes. The I is creative, turned outward, while the ego is possessive, turned inwards. The I knows itself through its capacity to create awareness. The ego knows itself through the desire to feel its own awareness, the desire for self-feeling, which must come from the outside. Because it comes from the outside, this feeling can never be guaranteed, and when had it lasts only for a short time and has to be repeated endlessly. This is what makes the ego by its very nature an addict. Self-love, seen from the side of the I, on the other hand, is nothing more than a description of the operation of the I in its awareness of others and the world; that is to say, self-love is self-consciousness that encompasses the world. What then determines whether self-consciousness is turned creatively toward the world or addictively toward feeling itself?

The ego is always oriented toward the past, trying to hold on to what it has received from the past. It acts like a "finished" structure of consciousness, one that is complete; but since it is really not complete, it must continually seek affirmation that it is by acting like an *is* rather than a *becoming*. The I lives as an orientation toward the time current from the future, and thus knows only awareness, but not an awareness of itself. The ego is habitual, repetitive, and uncreative. The I can be imagined as a capacity rather than an entity, functions through improvisation, has no fixed form, and creates what it knows.

Conscious life takes place in the dynamic polarity of these two qualities of self-consciousness. Fear that comes with the experience of grieving can shift the polarity in the direction of the ego, while love shifts the polarity in the direction of the I. Thus, in the present time, egotism weighs heavily, and is bound to predominate unless we can find a balancing factor—which can only come out of recognizing that the element of love is what makes human consciousness possible in the first place.

In other words, a strengthening of love is needed within consciousness. This strengthening must come from within consciousness and not from the outside, which then would be a strengthening of the ego. Such a strengthening can come about only indirectly, through learning to work with fear and grieving.

Soul Boredom and Fear

The self-enclosed ego remains closed by combating anything new that tries to enter. Discomfort, uneasiness, and fear are felt when the ego is faced with the unfamiliar, for the ego operates on the basis of old conceptions. It is possible to get along and even enjoy life on the basis of thoughts that have already been thought, feelings that have already been felt, and actions that have become habitual—as long as these ways of living from the past are continually verified by what one faces in the world. As long as living in time was based on the stream from the past, it was possible to live from the ego. The situation becomes critical, however, when nothing coming from without is familiar, when it looks as if the world is changing from day to day, for the ego then does not know what to do except to shut itself off from the outer course of time.

However, as we have seen, we have entered a time when the soul realm is no longer sharply divided from the realm of consciousness. The conjoining of soul with consciousness brings about a longing for new impressions, for soul longs for impressions from the time current of the future. The ego suffers a confusion because it seeks the comfort of the known while at the same time soul desires the new. This confusion defines the inner state of boredom. One feels boredom when there is a desire for new experiences, while at the same time new experiences are not allowed to enter. I feel bored when I want to do something but do not know what to do because the prospect of doing something really new threatens old conceptions. Boredom may be the primary malady of the age.

Boredom makes us prey for the amplification of fear, since fear inserts us into a world in which nothing familiar can be relied upon. In the presence of such unfamiliarity, the desire for new experiences—but only for experiences that can be counted on— takes the form of addictions. An addiction consists of something —whether a substance, another person, power, love, money, practically anything in the world—that momentarily relieves soul boredom in a way that seems to offer new experiences that can be controlled. Even drug addiction offers this possibility of experiencing release from the boundedness of the ego, but in such a way that the doorway to the experience of the I is not opened.

Drug addiction may seem to be a prime example of loss of control, exemplary of all addictions as loss of control. Addictions, however, are conditions of a completely controlled loss of control. Here, fear is met by utilizing something known to satisfy the longing for new impressions—another love, another bet at the racetrack, a hit, more money, power—which brings a momentary

intensity of experience that acts as a substitute for the truly new
and unknown.

As long as the central phenomenon of soul now seeking to
enter the conscious domain is not seen, a cure for an addiction
can only become another addiction. The longing of soul for impressions from the time current from the future can be satisfied in
a healthy way only through the central fact of self-consciousness
being the same thing as self-love. Through self-love, love enters
now into the quality of conscious soul life. Thus, the result of soul
becoming conscious in the I, and of the functioning of the I being
love, is that only I and I alone can work on myself to turn self-
love toward others and the world. Rudolf Steiner indicates that
this is the case: "Love must turn to the self, only in order to turn
the self into service in the world; the rose adorns herself only in
order to adorn the garden."

Here, we have a hint concerning the nature of self-love—one
that must be looked at carefully, for Steiner's words are carefully
chosen. He says that love turns to the self, and that makes possible a transmuting of self into service in the world. He does not say
that the self is turned toward service in the world, but that love of
self can "turn the self into service in the world." Love is the act of
serving, but in such a manner that no distinction is made between
the I who is serving and the activity of serving. As long as a distinction is made, a separation exists between myself and the world.
While that sense of separation persists, service is something that
the ego does in the world for some real or imagined, tangible or
intangible, material or spiritual reward—it is not the world's activity taking place through my presence.

I am not only an entity that does something in the world, but
also the Earth's consciousness individualized. At the same time,
Earth's consciousness is not the obliteration of the full individuality of the I. To serve, to love, does not mean to dissolve into some

kind of mystical unity with the Earth; rather, we are here taken into the mystery of Earth as love. Earth is in the process of individualizing itself, over a vast amount of time, through humanity become fully conscious and individualized.

The following chapter explores one way of consciously working to turn self-consciousness toward the world, a way in which we can work toward strengthening the subtle body through conscious work with dreams. This way of working with dreams is not concerned with dream interpretation or with getting to know oneself better, but rather is oriented toward showing the quality of turning oneself to service in and for the world.

6

DREAMING AND THE WORLD

DEPTH PSYCHOLOGY relies a great deal on dreams as the royal road to experiencing the reality of soul. In what follows I also shall till this rich soil, but from an angle that relates them with the themes at hand—the necessity of finding our way into the time current from the future, developing toward individuality, awakening the body as in-soul, and sensing the world as soul activity. I shall not here develop a new method of dream analysis, though some indications of a new way of working with dreams will be given. Instead, I shall concentrate on looking into the nature of dream images at the moment of their coming into being. Much has been overlooked here because the emphasis in dreams has been either on showing how dream images are expressions of archetypal realities—gods, goddesses, and spirits of the past—or on trying to use dreams to fortify the isolated sense of the ego, by showing how dream images often express traumas from the past, which, when made conscious can then be overcome.

Dream Content and Dream Activity

Anyone at all interested in dreams must acknowledge Sigmund Freud as the modern founder of dreamwork. *The Interpretation of Dreams* stands as his classic to which all further work is consciously or unconsciously indebted. The basic premise of this work is that dreams are not just chaotic leftovers from experiences of the day, but that every dream means something. Since Freud, almost no one has questioned this premise; the questions have all concerned where to locate meaning and how to go about understanding it. For Freud, meaning is to be found in relation to the waking life of the dreamer, particularly the personal past which dreams present in disguised and symbolic form. For Jung, meaning resides not only in relation to the personal past, but more importantly in relation to the realm of the archetypes of the collective unconscious.

The work of James Hillman has come closest to suggesting that meaning is not the only way to approach dreamwork. For Hillman, the importance of dreams is to be found in the metaphorical quality of images which can educate us into the laws of imagination and the spontaneous image-making that is characteristic of the soul. The important question for Hillman is not meaning, but value, the value of depth, soul, inwardness, and archetypal imagination rather than reified archetypes. Hillman's insights make possible going even further by emphasizing that value is not just another approach to meaning, but takes us from meaning into doing; that is to say, dreams not only mean something, but do something. The basis for what follows is this question: What do dreams do?

The question of the actual activity of dreaming has received little attention because all dream work emphasizes the content of dreams, taking content to be either symbolic, as in the case of Freud and Jung, or metaphorical, as in the case of Hillman. Here again, Hillman has made a true advance because he does not imply that dreams indicate anything outside of what they are in themselves; dreams are not metaphors for something else, but a different reality, a metaphorical reality. Nonetheless, whether one works to get at something behind the manifest content or takes the content to be all there is and realizes that this content has to be revisioned as an imaginal reality, content remains the center of interest. The reason, I want to suggest, that content remains the center of interest is that in turning to dream reality, the content of the world is turned away from and yet, inadvertently, world content is relied upon.

By world content I mean simply that, upon awakening from sleep, dream images at first seem to present themselves in ways that are not entirely unfamiliar to us; pictures are presented that in one way or another resemble the waking world in which we live. Even the most fantastic dreams seem to present themselves as if they had to do with the world with which we are familiar. That is to say, dreams seem to present themselves as if they were appearances of the day world. Even if I dream of something so fantastic as a fly-ing dragon with six horns and eight eyes that lives in a cave on the surface of the moon, it is still possible to describe the image in rec-ognizable terms because its individual elements resemble something physical, whether or not these things actually exist.

If we look more closely at what happens when we wake up from sleep and remember a dream, something of how the already-known world becomes involved in the dream becomes apparent. While we sleep the activity of dreaming occurs. This activity, I shall show, does not resemble the world that we know. We wake up and remember a dream. Perhaps we then write down the dream in a journal. In proceeding from the dreaming activity to the writ-ing of the dream, we are twice removed from the actual dreaming. First, there is the memory of the dream upon awakening. Then the memory of the dream is put into a narrative or a story. The dream is made to live in the world of waking life in this process. As this translation occurs, activity is turned into an understand-able content.

Further, this world content obscures the experience of the activ-ity of the dreaming. Whenever we try to write down a dream, or even when we wake up and remember a dream, we always feel that something has escaped, that what we remember or what we write down does not fully capture what happened in the night. The kind of dream work to be described here has a primary interest in getting closer to the qualities of dream life that are felt as having escaped our attempts to fix them in memory or story.

The conversion of dream activity into memory and then into story cannot be said to be a completely arbitrary making of content. We not only remember dreams, we also remember something of what it was like to be dreaming. Here, however, content is far more mobile, less fixed, and has a stronger element of coming into being rather than already having been. The quality of a dream as it is coming into being, dream as activity, lights up a content. The lighting up, however, is essentially different from *what* is lighted up. What is lighted up belongs to the processes of the etheric or subtle body and emulates what exists in the world of the senses during waking life.[1] This emulation of the sense world is readily converted into memory and story in forms that resemble the waking world.

To say all of this in a more ordinary way, what we speak of as a dream consists of invisible yet tangible activity that weaves into the living substance of the body, the life of the body which contains all of the thoughts, fantasies, and memories ever experienced, in full or partial consciousness, or even below the threshold of conscious awareness. Insofar as dream work focuses on content, much can indeed be learned concerning what has occurred in the past that is relevant to one's life, either in a personal or collective sense. But, what is coming to be—*that* has much more to do with the invisible weaving activity that *lights up* the content. How is it possible to give attention to this element of dream life?

As I hope is becoming apparent, we are in pursuit of the creating activity of dream life, which tends to be neglected because it is usually confused with what is created. This creating element gives dreams the mysterious quality that makes dream work so attractive. Yet, this element is lost in all interpretation of dreams as personal content and is given away with all archetypal approaches to dreams, which come to the brink of recognizing its importance but then relinquish it by calling this creating element the work of the gods. Approaching dreams for personal meaning makes our personal past stronger and more important than what I want to focus on—that is, what we might become by taking responsibility for creating. Approaching dreams for their archetypal significance all too quickly hands over individual creating to religious sentiment and deprives us of the capacity for an ongoing, collaborative creativity with the world.

Bypassing the creating element of dreaming has great significance. If this element is missed in working with dreams, where it is most strongly revealed, then it is also going to be missed in all other psychic activity. The ability of this activity to create gradually decreases through a continuum of psychic activity in the following manner: dream—fantasy—memory—thinking—perception. Creating activity is strongest with the dream, for there it is most free. This element is still present in fantasy, although more bound to the ego (the ego is always at the center of our fantasy life, with imaginary pictures serving the wishes of the ego). With memory a creating element is still present, but is now bound to an event that occurred in the outer world. Thus, memory recalls events that have happened, but does not do this in a completely literal way. With thinking, the creating element is bound to the laws of logic, which bring an orderly relation between one thought and another; when this orderly element is lacking, we have something approaching free association rather than thinking. And, with perception, the creating element is most bound, for what we perceive in the world is bound by what is actually present before us. Nonetheless, even in perception there is an aspect of creating what we see, as evidenced by the possibility of illusion.

To feel the ongoing unity of the I with the world, we need to be able to consciously experience the presence of creating going on in the full range of psychic life. Dream work can be a significant way of strengthening the creative force of the I. Strengthening the sensing of creating does not bring about a disjunction between psychic life and the capacity to experience the world, but rather brings about a more vivid experience of the world as every moment coming into being rather than as already completed. This experience, further, is not due to imposing private and subjective creating onto the world; it is due to developing the capacity to be present to the creating action of the world through sensing this same kind of action within. That is, strengthening the conscious experience of psychic life as creative strengthens the organs needed to perceive this same kind of creating going on in the world.

Dreaming and the Strengthening of the I

Everything we have ever experienced in life, even things that have escaped consciousness, are remembered by the body—not in the brain, but in the life of the body itself. The body is more than physiological organs and material processes. Time lives in the body; not only time past, but, in a certain way, time future. The etheric body is the time substance of the body. Clairvoyants can perceive the etheric body and can see the future possibilities coming to be. This kind of clairvoyance is not a spiritual ability but rather an enhanced sensory capacity.

Lived time, the time of the body, may be described as memoria, presentness, and possibility—seen, however, as a unified whole. Dreams can thus be approached as a border phenomenon, meaning that they at one and the same time picture something of the past waking life of the dreamer and something of the life of soul and spirit coming into the world. When dreams are approached in terms of their content, we are taken in the direction of how the past is affecting the individual life of the person in the world. When dreams are approached not as a content, but as an activity, then we are taken toward the direction of the creating activity of the I in its unity with the creating activity that is the world.

To get a clearer sense of this picture-weaving activity, we must try to get a feeling for the process of dreaming. I go to sleep at night. There, lying on the bed is my physical body. But, in addition, there, lying on the bed is a living body—etheric body processes go on. But consciousness is not there. Where has it gone? Consciousness is an activity of soul, the overlapping of the time current from the past with the time current from the future. Individuality of consciousness is an activity of the I. At night, when we are asleep, these two aspects of our being have commerce in the soul and spirit worlds. Then, either in the morning, or at some time during the night when I come close to waking, soul and the I again unite more closely with the physical body and the etheric body, and as they do so, they light up the etheric body with a weaving activity of picture-making.

If we try to work with our dreams in the direction of their activity rather than their content, then we can get a feeling of the life of the soul and the I weaving into the etheric body. To work in this way requires recognizing that an image has a logic different than the logic of the day world. When I write down a dream in the morning, I transfer this night logic into the logic of the day world. I make the dream seem as if it were a sequence of events happening one after the other. But the sequence of events is due to my translation of the image into a form to be written down.

How would we approach a dream in terms of the logic of an image, not the logic of an event in the day world? Take a simple dream, such as: "I am climbing up the side of a very steep mountain. As I ascend, the green growth of grass and flowers and trees disappears, and all becomes solid rock. I climb out onto a rock ledge, and the ground behind me falls away, and I am left on a ledge overlooking an abyss with no way to get back. I wake in fear." An analyst might look at this dream and say that I am living too high, or trying too hard to get to the top, or perhaps that I am afraid of getting to the top, where I will be on my own. A more soul-oriented depth psychologist might say that when I am too egotistical I have to suffer the fear of facing the abyss; the dream is trying to balance my too one-sided view of things.

An approach to dreaming as activity would begin with seeing that the whole dream is an image, and that an image happens all at once, not in sequence. Just as one part of the image in a painting cannot be said to occur before another part, so also with dreaming. Thus, when I am climbing, there is the abyss; when there is the abyss, then I am out on a ledge; when there is no way back, then things have gotten steep and rocky; I feel rocky when the abyss appears; the abyss appears when greening disappears; high moving loses greenness; being high is rocky going. Here, there is no interpretation, only the work of feeling the weaving.

As the dream story is moved back toward dream image from which it came, interest in what the dream means begins to dissolve; I am taken away from meaning toward doing. At this point, however, we have come closer to the content existing now as part of the processes of the etheric body. Here the dream image lives as duration of the whole rather than as a sequence of events that seem to occur one after another. The dream as image occurs all at once. Only as we are awaking does this simultaneity of the whole image begin to feel like a sequence of events. We remember dreams in the process of waking. Usually, dreaming that occurs prior to the transition to waking cannot be remembered, though we remember that we have in fact dreamed, and have a feeling of the dream as a whole, which nonetheless cannot be recollected.

If we go only this far in working with dreams, we come to the metaphorical reality of image, which is as far as James Hillman has taken his exploration of the phenomenology of dream life. This kind of work is valuable and is not to be bypassed. The dream has changed from something like a sequential story which invites interpretation to an image which we observe as a whole thing going on at once. Here we discover an interesting aspect of dream interpretation: Interpretation is actually a defense against the dream. With the dream, we come up against a different sense of reality. This reality is at the same time compelling and frightening.

Interpretation is a compromise that allows one to have some sense of this different reality without risking losing hold of what one already holds to be reality. But, by working with the image quality of dreaming we begin to lose the firm hold on the world as already known. To go any further requires a kind of courage—not a heroic attempt to enter into the unknown and conquer what is found there, but what can be spoken of as spiritual courage to leave the ego behind and enter into not-knowing, which is deeper even than metaphorical knowing.

Once we have a feeling for the dream as an image that is happening all at once, the next step is to imaginatively "step into" the image, a little like Alice going through the looking glass. To get a feeling for what this is like, imagine standing before a painting. Once you are able to put aside the fact that you are standing in a room in a museum and looking at a framed picture on a wall, and begin to be intensely interested in the painting itself, the painting comes alive. Everything in the painting relates to everything else; you experience the whole, which is different than paint on a canvas.

Now, imagine stepping into the painting in such a way that as you do you no longer feel yourself to be at a location in space with the rest of the painting around you; instead, your consciousness is everywhere within the painting. Since you are no longer looking *at* the painting, the image disappears. What remains are only qualities of motion, of movement, of tension, of ups and downs, of sweeping color. When we do this with a dream image, we move from image into activity. This activity can be felt as a kind of consciousness of pure mobility and creation coming into being. This mobility has distinct characteristics that vary from one dream to another, so that we are not dissolving into amorphous movement but are very close to the creating activity of the I, which will be different with every dreaming activity. Presence within this activity can now be brought to expression by trying to write as directly as possible what is felt. This writing always comes forth as something like a poem, though constructing poetry is not the object of the exercise. The dream example we have followed thus far can be expressed in the following way:

Dream Story

I am climbing up the side of a very steep mountain. As I ascend, the green growth of grass and flowers and trees disappears, and all becomes solid rock. I climb out onto a rock ledge, and the ground behind me falls away, and I am left on a ledge overlooking an abyss with no way to get back. I wake in fear.

Dream Image

When I am climbing, then there is the abyss; when there is the abyss, then I am out on a ledge; when there is no way back, then things have gotten steep and rocky; I feel rocky when ledge and life have disappeared; the greening, growing, flowering disappears when I feel rocky; I am at an abyss when greening disappears; high moving loses greenness; being high is rocky-going fear.

Dream Activity

Climbing overlooks the void
a ledge of no return
green, flowering growth, an abyss
steeped in fear—I am.

The dream activity can be expressed in many ways. Or it need not be expressed in an outer form at all, just felt. This activity does not mean anything other than what it is. I do not know what it tells me about my life, for the point of this work isn't to "get"

anything from the dreaming, but rather to get ever closer to the
activity. The point is also not about "having an experience," or
becoming a poet or an artist, or turning to aesthetics or anything
else. This sort of dream work strengthens the creating sense of the
I, and that is all. Seekers and questers are likely to feel disappointed,
but imagine working with dreams this way over time. Let me give
another example.

Dream Story

I am lecturing to a class. As I stand in front of the group, I
notice what appears to be white cotton on my left index finger.
I start to pull on the cotton and realize that it is coming out of
a wound in my finger. As I pull the cotton out, it turns into a
string of deep purple-red beads, like prayer beads. I look at this
happening in amazement.

Dream Image

When lecturing to a class, then my pointing finger turns to cotton. When my finger is wounded, then cotton appears. When
in front of class, beads of purple-red appear at my finger. I am
amazed when lecturing. As I point out things, it is like pray-
ing. Lecturing points out my wounds in the form of prayer.

Dream Activity

Standing in amazement
　speaking to a class
what is inside appears fluffy white
one rounded form after another
　wounds like prayer strung at finger tip
unexpected purple-red vulnerability.

Working with dreams in such a way, we gradually become more
conscious of ourselves as creating beings who can bring our creating into conjunction with the world. We are consciously exercising

the same kind of activity that creates dreaming. We can also practice such exercises in relation to fantasy, memory, thinking, and perception and find that we are also involved in creating their content. The world also then begins to have similar qualities of coming into being, for this work develops the capacity to experience the world as advent rather than event. We realize more clearly, however, that the world as advent can be forgotten and lost unless we do our part.

From Dream Activity to World Activity

Part of the value of working with dreaming as activity concerns attentiveness to things that cannot be used, but which are of the utmost value because they concern the whole of our being and are entered into with the whole of our being. The kind of dream work described above can be a training for entering into the world with the whole of our being. The world of objects around us is not so reliable as we would believe. Only because we are so unobservant does this world seem fixed. As long as the I remains unnoticed, the world appears relatively the same; but through strengthening the sense of the I, the world begins to show forth constant nuances of change.

Suppose I look out my window at the landscape every day. Because of the constant change of light and shadow, of clouds and sun, of mist and wind, objects change shape, distance, and group themselves differently at different times. A tree that at one time may be the central figure, at another time is part of the background. Coloring may vary from bluish to silver white to shades of indigo and purple. The world, like the dream, is constantly coming into being in different ways; it is ever new.

If we were to come upon the soul qualities of the world without preparation, we would be overwhelmed. Strengthening the I makes possible presence to the ever-changing qualities of the world in such a way that each single change is felt in relation to the whole. Apparently separate impressions are threads in a multitudinous interweaving. A single plant, for example, cannot be separated from its whole setting in a landscape, the sun, moon, and stars, the moisture and the earth, the accompanying life of birds, animals, and insects. The world ordinarily appears to us as a content. We must work to come to experience it as an image in which everything is in relation with everything else.

Different, ongoing experiences of the world are like individual dreams; each experience, nonetheless gives a sense of the whole. Then, we must make the further step of realizing that we are not only part of the whole but are also responsible for our share of the creating process. This responsibility is even greater in terms of the human-made aspects of the world. Here it is more difficult because so much of the human world has been made as disconnected fragments due to self-interests. This fragmentation cannot be turned around in a short time, but work in this area begins through relationships with others who are also longing for the restoration of a whole world and have made the decision to work in the world toward this end. How might one go about this kind of work in the world? I want to approach this question in relation to what has been said concerning dreams.

The main attribute of dream work of the sort just described is a concern for working with dreams in a healthy way. It is healthy because a conscious method was established that follows what ordinarily occurs when we go to sleep. As stated before, when we fall asleep, the physical body, which is also the living body of life processes, lies there on the bed. Ordinary consciousness is no longer present, and the individuality of our consciousness is also not present. We cannot say simply that we are unconscious, for dreams reveal that a kind of consciousness is involved that is unlike ordinary waking consciousness. I have described this consciousness as pure mobility, movement, flow, shaping. Little more than this can be said about it. It is not the same as dream pictures, but more like the activity within and between the pictures.

An analogy would be the relation between the substance and the activity of the body. My arm, for example, can be described as of the substance of flesh. My arm can also be described in terms of its activity, as when I move my arm to reach for something. Substance and activity are interwoven. I place the emphasis with dream work on activity in order to develop the capacity to experience the world of dream consciousness as of a decidedly different quality than the world we experience in ordinary waking consciousness. This same kind of activity is also always weaving into world content, but we are not capable of experiencing it without first strengthening our capacity to do so.

When we work with dreams in the manner described, we begin with the dream as it has been expressed in ordinary consciousness—what could be called the physical body of the dream. Then we work to get a feeling for the dream-as-image, what could be called the life process of the dream. Finally we work to get a sense of the dream-as-activity, what could be called the soul and spirit of the dream. This procedure is like consciously following the process of going into sleep.

We can also look at the process in the reverse direction. When we are asleep, soul and spirit are engaged in their own environment. As we are slowly coming out of sleep, soul and spirit weave into the life processes of the body, lighting up a dream content. When we wake, this content is put into forms of ordinary consciousness. Developing a procedure to follow this natural process makes for healthy dream work that can work its way into the world.

If no attention is given to this process and one dives right down into dreams with procedures such as free association, dream interpretation, or active imagination, or goes directly to the dream material by examining the images, much can be learned; but the dream activity cannot find its way into the world. The difference

between the usual procedures of depth psychology and the one out-
lined here is this: The former, in effect, abstract the dream from its
context; the latter recognizes the dream as belonging to the context of sleep. I am more of a researcher of sleep than of dreams.
The difference between a researcher of sleep and a researcher of
dreams has to do with recognizing the importance of rhythm, the
inseparable rhythm of waking and sleeping. The quality of rhythm
has a great deal to do with the question posed earlier: How can one
go about working in the world to restore the sense of the unity of
the whole? First, two observations concerning sleep are important.

One observation is that sometimes when we wake from sleep,
often after a nap rather than night sleep, upon the moment of waking we feel a peculiar sensation. This sensation is somewhat
difficult to describe, but it is something like feeling a strong wind
rushing into the body, a whoosh, a coming back into the physical
body. This sensation can also sometimes be felt at the conclusion
of meditation. This sensation verifies much of what has been stated
about the process of going into sleep and coming back to the waking state. We do not just go unconscious and eight hours later
become conscious again; sleep and waking are a rhythmical process
in which they exist together as phases of a whole.

The second observation is that if we learn to be as conscious as
possible at the moment of waking, we find that we always wake up
with a certain mood. This mood is simply there and usually cannot be related to anything we may be feeling in the course of
waking life. One may wake feeling joy, or sorrow, or slight depression, or many other specific moods. We do not wake up neutral.
The mood upon waking is more than a feeling or an emotion. The
mood has a moral quality to it. This moral quality has nothing to
do with a conventional sense of morality, but it is a feeling with a
certain quality of prompting about it. This ever-so-slight urging, it
seems to me, concerns the possibility of dream activity moving
into the world. We are not forced in any way to become consciously

creative in the world, drawing from the resources of the night; it comes upon us more as an invitation to do so. If such an invitation can be openly listened to, then development of the close unity between the I and the soul can bring about a conscious, individual, soul approach to the world.

We may now ask why this process does not occur naturally without our having to take up such a subtle work. Why does not dream activity find its way naturally into the world? The unity between the I and the soul is natural to the processes of the night and dreaming. Here both factors are together. But, as soon as they return from their nightly sojourn and reenter bodily life, the I is obscured by the strong presence of the ego. Less so, soul is obscured by having to wear the clothing of resemblances from the waking life of the dreamer. The former, however, seems to be the primary factor.

For example, in dream images, almost always present is the dream ego, the presence of ourselves in the dream either as an actual dream figure or as an observing consciousness. This presence is not the I, but the ego—ourselves as we know ourselves to be from the past, not what we are becoming. Thus, what remains of the soul's journey in the night is really only the detectable dream activity we cannot quite remember and the slight prompting of the morning. Work is therefore needed if these qualities are not to be overshadowed by the waking world.

Yet another factor is involved in the rhythmical relation between sleep and waking that requires attention: the physical body. The movement from dream activity to soul activity in the world is hampered greatly because our physical body now interferes with the rhythm rather than being a part of it. There are all sorts of reasons for this: the food we eat, the water we drink, the polluted environments in which we now live, the drugs we take, the tensions we live. All of these agents work against the capacity to experience the body being replenished nightly by the soul realm.

The soul is never out of order, but it can be disrupted from functioning as it should through bodily disturbance. Anyone who has taken the time and effort to really listen to someone who suffers from psychological disturbances quickly finds out that the fantasies, memories, thoughts, and perceptions of such a person make perfect sense in themselves, even in instances such as schizophrenia and paranoia. One is in fact always left with the impression of listening to a quite creative individual. This creativity, however, is for naught because it does not relate to the waking world, and the medium of such relationship is the body. If there is disturbance in the body, then the rhythm from night to day is disrupted.

I am not here siding with psychiatry which reduces psychic activity to brain functioning. The bodily disturbance can as well be centered in the liver, kidneys, lungs, heart, or any other organ. Further, an organ does not have be diseased to be functioning out of harmony with the whole body; it is sufficient for it to be overactive or underactive, out of balance. But, it is not just the schizophrenics and paranoids whose bodies are out of balance; the body of the world is out of balance and we all live this in our individual way with our bodies.

For all of the reasons stated, dream activity cannot naturally enter into the world. Nor can we assume that if we work on our bodies first—through cleaning them of their toxins, balancing them with massage and acupuncture, drinking bottled water, and eating natural foods—the situation would be improved very much. We also cannot assume that meditation and spiritual disciplines which would decrease the dominance of the ego would be the answer. Doing all of these things is of course beneficial, but the largest factor of all is choice. One must consciously choose to work to bring sleep and waking into a rhythmic whole.

Under present world conditions that recognize only the importance of the day world, such a choice is also a conscious sacrifice.

The word *sacrifice* means "to make holy," to make whole. We are required to give up what we might want for ourselves that makes life seem easier, more comfortable, more secure, more acceptable, more understandable. And, there is no tangible personal reward for doing so. In addition, the results of such a choice might well not even be evident within one's life. Thus, we are confronted with the very large question: Why make such a choice?

A choice to work toward becoming a fully conscious creator of the world has to be made completely freely. If such a choice is made because it may seem that the whole world will collapse unless we take on this task, this is really veiled egotism. Fear would be guiding the choice, and thus the decision is not free. If the choice is made because it can be seen that a better world would result, this is also veiled egotism because it is oriented toward a result that one would like to see come about. Noble choices are always easily captured by self-interests, even if at first they seem altruistic.

The choice to work in such a manner is a matter of love and an interest, though not a self-interest, in the phenomenon of love in the world; it is a kind of research into the activity of love. Of course, all of the senses of love explored in this writing are a basis for this interest; but this kind of love is different from all of the other kinds of love. I choose to work in this way because I choose to love in order to see love work and see what it can do, without really knowing what it can do.

The choice to love is the choice to try to extend the boundaries of this phenomenon as far as they can possibly go. It is an experiment, probably one without an end. From what we have said about love thus far, something of the nature of this experiment can be proposed. We have explored love as an urge, a force in the blood, an emotion, a knowledge of oneself, an action of the heart, and as a world phenomenon. The next part of the exploration, the one we are touching upon here, is love as a force in the world. This is love that goes beyond warm feelings, sentiment, attraction, commitment, and connection. Here we touch upon a mysterious force among people as the essence of the world itself, its substance, being, activity and destiny. I am quite certain that there are many, many people in the world who wish to work to serve this experiment.

Love is such an interesting phenomenon because it is so large and so small, and it is essentially the same power in both its immensity and its individual particularity. Thus, this experiment can be served in the smallest of ways, which are at the same time its largest dimensions. To take up the work of paying attention to nightly dream life is really a very small thing to do. I do not want to say that, nonetheless, this small act has large consequences, because its consequences are at one with the small acts themselves.

If we were to work in small ways and then wait, looking around for the consequences, we would be missing the peculiar way in which this phenomenon works. The phenomenon of love works in such a way that the small acts *are* the big consequences. That is to say, the smallest acts of love each encompass the whole world. The I is the act of love individualized—as particular as each individual, and as encompassing as the world.

We perhaps need to distinguish between the force of love and our expectations surrounding love. We tend to think that if love were practiced everything would be harmonious without effort. But, just as working to bring dream activity into the world is a constant effort and not something once and for all achieved, so love is about a new kind of work rather than the cessation of work. Soul work is actually more difficult than physical or mental work. This is so first because it is effort in the realm of the invisible, and second because the more that is done, the harder one must continue to strive. Creating is full-time work with no pay and no retirement.

7

COMING TO
OUR SENSES

THROUGH soul work, a sensitizing of the body gradually occurs, bringing about clearer, more vivid perception of the world. A radical disjunction becomes apparent between the world as it is now being made by human beings and what the Earth is from its own side. This disjunction and ways to begin healing it are what I would now like to consider.

Healing is not possible unless we can maintain conscious, bodily connection with the Earth. So we must start with the recognition that this connection is nearly severed; here is where healing must begin. I am not saying that we must first heal ourselves and then go about the task of making a more whole relation with Earth. Nor am I saying that we must forget ourselves and turn now toward healing the Earth. The first of these alternatives is the way of depth psychology and of therapeutic psychology in general. The second alternative is the way of ecology. Here, I want to concentrate further on the connection itself—what goes on between the human being and the Earth, the meeting of individual soul and World Soul. What was said in chapter 5 about the subtle body must now be extended to include the individual body senses.

Imagination and Counter-Creation

Our senses have been disrupted by the making of a world independent of the Wisdom of the wider world, Sophia. Experiencing the necessary painfulness of grieving and coming closer to the actual creating activity that works through dreaming must be accompanied by working to be conscious of the wisdom of the senses. First, let us give attention to how we have lost our senses.

We do not readily perceive the world slipping into Chaos from day to day because a simulated world is continually being counter-created which often makes it seem as if a new world is in the making. Indeed it is, a world best described by the current term *virtual reality*. I extend the term, however, to include vastly more than the capacity to take information and make it into an experience through computer simulation. Electronic technology of this sort constitutes an exemplary instance of the counter-creating that happens whenever a simulation of any sort replaces immediate bodily presence to the world's body. Any symbol system qualifies, from language to thinking, to making theories to making art. However, an additional element is needed in order to counter-create, something more than just inserting a system of mediation between oneself and the world. Counter-creation occurs whenever sensations produced by a mediating medium between the body and the world produce effects that confuse the sensations usually brought about by an immediate bodily presence to the world.

The list of examples is vast and extremely varied. William Irwin Thompson has written extensively about the simulated world in *The American Replacement of Nature*.[1] Television and movies are prime instances. With these media, it is possible to produce sensations of desire in the body in the presence of images that are horrible and revolting. Why are obscene and pornographic images of violence not met with repugnance and revulsion so strongly felt that one is compelled to get up and leave when they are presented on the screen, never to return? Instead, a desire for more is produced; where there should be fear and revulsion, there is excitement.

I am not saying that violence in the media is the problem; the relative absence of a true imagination of violence is more to the point. Nor am I saying that the media, by their very nature are the source of the problem—that the solution is to be found in staying away from movies and television. The confusion of sensations is now found everywhere in the world, and it does not matter whether or not one has direct exposure. What occurs through the media is no more than an intensification of a worldwide phenomenon, from which there is no escape and no respite.

When imagination is presented in the world for us to experience without the conscious effort of individual imagination, then we are in the presence of counter-creation. Often, we go to the movies or watch television as if we were entering a dreamlike sleep. We go to the box office, purchase a ticket, and hand over our senses to the attendant; or we turn on the television, settle back into a chair and enter into a dullness of consciousness. These situations, further, are no more than intensified instances of similar occurrences that more or less define life in the world of counter-creation.

Is waking up and going to work in a large corporation not a similar handing over of one's individual consciousness? Is paying tuition, entering college, going to lectures where there may be one or two hundred students in a class really any different from paying to have one's imagination shaped from the outside? Is going to church to be preached to concerning what a church defines as its doctrine really any different from being manipulated in the guise of goodness? Is reading a book that does not require grappling with what is said, even if it makes one feel good, any different from more of the above? Nothing is demanded of one who goes to a movie other than paying the fee. Nothing is demanded of the television viewer other than sitting down. Nothing is demanded of the visitor to Disney World other than subjecting oneself to the experience. In these instances, imaginary worlds are presented as sense experiences. It is as if a dream comes from the outside, except that it is not really a dream at all, but a sense experience acting like a dream world.

Imagination has entered the realm of fully waking consciousness. It has become an ever-present constituent of waking life, but without our being aware that this indeed is the case. We are being assaulted by sense-bound imagination all of the time. But, as long as the I is not aware of itself as a creating, improvising, giving activity without content, as long as the I still continues to function as the ego, this form of imagination has the power to put the ego to sleep. When the ego is asleep, there is no way to distinguish what is being presented to the senses from dreaming.

The confusion of sensations brought about through presenting already-formed imaginations to the ego that has not broken through to the experience of the activity of the I can be readily described. When the ego is presented with images which it does not have a part in creating, such images have the appearance of something between the imaginary and the real. They are pictures of sense experiences disguised as images, neither true sense experiences nor true imagination. Seeing a bear out in the wild, for example, is not a comparable experience to seeing a bear in a zoo. Seeing a bear in the zoo is not unlike watching a wildlife movie. In the former instance, seeing a bear in the mountains, there is a complete context of perception that engages all of the senses and also calls forth the activity of imagination. In the latter instance, the context has been narrowed and made safe and comfortable, so that the senses perceive dully; what is actually seen is a simulation of a bear, an image of a bear that is more like a fantasy bear than an actual bear.

Seeing the suffering of people in war on the television news is not comparable to seeing this suffering through an immediate presence—the context is gone, and, as well, the smell, the taste, the feel, the touch, the whole tragic atmosphere. It is the difference between simulation and true imagination. Are we sensing what is there or being fed a sense-bound image? The kind of imaginings that result from hallucinogenic drugs, which obliterate even further the activity of the ego, cannot be said to be true experiences of imagination, but only simulations. The images of the planets received from satellites in space are not true images because they are mediated by constructions—satellites, rockets, space stations—inserted between the cosmos and the Earth; thus we have scientific, technological rendering of the planets, as if the device from which they are viewed makes no difference.

The ego, if presented with true images, say in the form of a great work of art, does not have the capacity to relate to true imagination, and perceives only nonsense. The I, on the other hand, encountering a great work of art, perceives that work through, in part, creating what is perceived. If the I views a masterful painting of a horse, something that is more than a representation of a horse, it perceives the power, movement, instinct, vitality, spirit, of the horse—all of which may only be suggested in the painting by a line or a color. Creative perception in alert consciousness is required to bring the painting to completion.

Further, when the I encounters images that require no participatory activity, it readily experiences them as false. However, since the ego and the I are the same function—in the former case directed inward and relying on the past, and in the latter case directed outward and oriented toward what is coming to be—living in a world pervaded by pre-formed images works strongly against the I developing its own imaginal capacities, and erodes such a capacity if it exists. Finding the mode of love that can bring balance to living in a simulated world, with its confusion of sensations, requires first an exploration of the relation of the body to the world of simulated imagination.

Counter-Creating the Body

In chapter 5, I spoke of how the etheric body of individuals and of the world is under attack by the force of radiation in the world, and how this force is also a devolution of human consciousness toward literalism. There we began to see that the soul is somewhat more complex than usually defined or circumscribed by psychologies of the soul life: that soul cannot be confined to the inner life of individuals, and that something like soul qualities belong to the essential activity of Earth. We also saw that Earth has her own depth, and that a distinct relation exists between the soul or psychic life of individuals and the Soul of the World. As we proceed, this complexity will have to be extended even further through connecting soul, sense experience, and the I.

First, it is to be noted that the propensity to become a consumer of images rather than an active imagining individual is due to the undeniable fact that it is far easier and more comfortable to be given images than to be involved in creating them. The imaginal I is creative, which means that at each moment it starts with practically nothing; the world comes every moment as a surprise; and every act of creating makes the next action all the more challenging, because the I must again start with practically nothing. Every true artist knows something of this experience.

A painter, for example, who paints one picture and then goes on to paint another, will find the second one more difficult to produce than the first, precisely because it is necessary to set aside what one has already accomplished. If this act of setting aside the previous accomplishment is not carried out, the second painting will not be a true creation, but an imitation or at the very most a variation of what was already completed. At the same time, the act of creating the first painting strengthens the soul forces, making it possible to go beyond what one has already done. Thus, it is not a matter of depleting one's resources, but rather of strengthening capacities. What the true artist is able to accomplish is very much like what it means to live from the time current from the future rather than from the time current from the past.

The mode of living from the future being described here may seem impossible, but it must be remembered that none of this should be thought of in terms of content; rather the picture-weaving activity of conscious soul life is what is important. Viewed from the outside, a person able to live in the direction of the time current from the future may appear to engage in the same actions day in and day out. Further, it is not a matter of what a person does; the content of the actions can range from the simplest activity, such as mopping floors, to a most complex activity such as scientific research. These activities can be no more than habitual acts based on what is already known, or they can every moment participate in the not-known.

Even though, to the untrained eye, whether someone lives from the past or from the future may not be visible, the effects in the world are unmistakably different. One way of living subtracts from the world, and the other adds immeasurably to its soul. In order to try and demonstrate that these differences are true and not a matter of accepting what might appear to be mystical belief, let us look into some particular aspects of the senses.

In considering the difference between consuming images and living consciously through the creating activity of the imaginal I, the crucial element is the part played by the senses. We are accustomed to thinking of the senses of the body as organs for receiving impressions of what the world has to offer. What we have been speaking of as the I, however, is also intimately involved in sensing, for it is possible to attend in a given situation to one of the senses while letting the others recede into the background. The I can, so to speak, circulate from one sense to another. But, ordinarily, the senses function together, not separately, and the part played by the I in synthesizing them goes unnoticed.

While psychology and physiology recognize, at the most, seven senses, Rudolf Steiner describes twelve senses. He relates each sense to a constellation of the zodiac, which in turn allows one to picture the circulation of the I through the senses like the sun moving through the constellations.[2] For our considerations, however, the most important aspect of sensing is the relation between the inner senses and the outer senses.

The inner senses inform us of the interior of the body in its ongoing relation to the world. The outer senses inform us of the world as it comes into connection with the body. There are five inner senses and seven outer senses. The five inner senses are touch, movement, the life sense, balance, and smell. The seven outer senses are sight, warmth, sound, taste, the word sense, the thinking sense, and the ego sense. The five senses described by Steiner that have yet to be discovered by physiology are the life sense, the warmth sense, the word sense, the thinking sense, and the ego sense. A short description of these senses is needed

The life sense senses the well-being or ill-being of the body. Perhaps I wake up in the morning and feel great; the next morning I may wake up feeling lousy. The capacity to sense this difference is due to the life sense, and the organs of perception here are the sympathetic and parasympathetic nerve systems. This sense also senses pain, hunger, thirst, fatigue, and feeling rested.

The warmth sense senses the relation between the temperature of the body and the temperature of the surroundings. The speech sense senses speech sounds made by another person—the movements of a speaker's larynx, tongue, and lips that shape a stream of sound into the forms of vowels and consonants. The speech sense does not sense the meaning of these sounds, only that there is a particular sounding of speech in the world. The thought sense does not refer to understanding what another person is thinking, but is the immediate sensing that another is thinking. The thought sense does not give us the content of a thought, but enables us to sense

that another person is thinking by the pattern of organized movement of a stream of speech sounds. The ego sense senses something
of the individuality of another person; it goes beyond the visual
appearance by sensing that a true individuality is facing us.

I will concentrate here on the inner senses, because they are the
most radically disrupted through the counter-creating of images to
be consumed. The outer senses are also disrupted, but more as a
result of this disruption of the interior of bodily life.

When images are matter for consumption, they are a forming
of material oriented primarily to the outer senses. Further, this
material typically requires that the inner senses become passive.
When I see a movie or watch television, for example, I sit motion-
less, eyes focused at an unchanging distance, the senses of movement and balance asleep. What seems to be relaxation is in fact a
dulling of the life sense; one does not feel refreshed or renewed
after watching television. If I am watching a scene of people climbing in the mountains, I smell nothing of the pine trees; and as they
camp out for the night, the smells of the campfire, the taste of the
food, the touch of the cool air have no part with me. The inner
senses have been converted into outer pictures. And in daily life,
images are presented at such a rapid pace—in news, information,
advertising, entertainment, work to be done, obligations to be met,
phones to answer, newspapers to read—it is virtually impossible to
experience the interior of the body in experiencing these things.
And, when the interior life of the body is not a constant experience, there can be no experience of soul, neither the individual soul
nor the Soul of the World. The inner senses are at the same time
a sensing of the soul.

The notion of soul remains a religious, pious, and abstract idea
from the past as long as it is not a complex of sensations felt deeply
within the body. And, if soul is not at the same time an experience of the body, there is no possibility of the individual soul
adding to the soul body of the world. Further, the ego remains

forever isolated as a spectator to the world unless worked upon by the inner senses; that is to say, *the change in function from an ego to an I depends upon an aliveness of the interior of the body.* Soul is body from the inside, an organ consciousness in which, through the inner sense of the body, the inner qualities of outer things can be felt. The sense of soul is obscured by religious notions which seek to convince us that soul is antithetical to body. When the body was abandoned by religion, the stage was set for counter-creation.

Recovering the Soul of the Inner Senses

The inner senses are crucial to accurate sensing. If we are in connection with the inner senses, then the outer senses are accurate. Virtual reality works because the inner senses are disrupted, making the outer senses subject to manipulation.

Each of the inner senses is also a particular soul quality. Touch, for example, is the sense that establishes a boundary between our body and the world. With touch, we experience ourselves as separate bodily beings and at the same time connected with what is not us. Touch is more than a mechanical or a physiological process— something else enters in addition to the stimulation of the nerves. We become conscious of our body through touch, and also conscious of what is not our body, both at the same moment.

If the sense of touch is disrupted, the boundary between what is us and what is other than us is obscured. Thus, if one is isolated in a sensory deprivation chamber, hallucinations arise; one no longer has a sense of body.

Touch is the basis for the soul experience of a longing for the divine because with this sense we feel separated from what is not us, and unable to enter it, but nonetheless in touch with it. The strong erotic quality of touch involves this longing for intimacy, the possibility of recovering unity. The essential character of pornography is to be found in the fact that the inner sense of touch is distanced and made into outer pictures. When the sense of touch is dulled or disrupted by being made into an outer picture, longing for the divine becomes no more than an abstract thought. The dulling of this sense also makes it seem that this boundary has been crossed, when it in fact has not. True spiritual experiences do not come about by dulling the senses, but through a strengthening of the senses.

The interior quality of the sense of touch can be strengthened by tactile visualizations—for example, imagining a scene such as walking in the woods, coming across something such as a large rock, touching the rock, and sensing what the moment of touching feels like. The inner sense of touching is not strengthened by doing sensitivity exercises, because the work is to become conscious *in* the senses, not conscious *of* the senses.

The sense of movement is the awareness, from within, of the movements of the body. If I move my arm, for example, there is an inner experience of that movement. This sense concerns not only the large movements of the body, but even the smallest, such as a motion of the eye. The organs for this sense are the nerves in connection with the muscle tissue of the body. The sense of movement makes possible moving from the immediacy of one experience of the world to another while retaining a sense of continuity of experience. That we do not experience the world one picture at a time and somehow have to put together multiple pictures to make a complete world is because of the sense of movement. The fact that we move about and our perception of the world is continually changing and yet we maintain a continuous sense of ourselves gives the feeling of a relatively independent soul life.

To feel what is most inside oneself, it is necessary at the same time to be most outside oneself. The sense of movement, when fully experienced, gives this experience, which is the basis for the experience of destiny, the particular qualities of the world as they are coming to meet us on our life path. Destiny is not a matter of information, something about our life that cannot be experienced. Only when the sense of movement is dulled do we go in search of our destiny, expecting that someone with psychic abilities can fill in this missing bit of information. Destiny is an ongoing sense quality, not information. A good exercise for strengthening this sense is to imagine walking, say, into the kitchen and seeing a glass of water on the table. Imagine reaching out to grasp the glass of water, but feel the glass of water coming to you as you reach out toward it.

The sense of balance gives us the ongoing feeling of our body in relation to the world. We keep our balance only in relation to something. Through this sense, the world appears steady and sure. Without this sense, the world would appear a little like what is seen when a movie camera bounces up and down; we would be constantly nauseous. The organ for balance is the inner ear. Balance is maintained in a gravitational field and expresses our relation to the solid Earth. When the sureness of the Earth is lost, as in traveling on the wavy ocean, we lose our balance.

The deeper quality of balance concerns what happens in this ongoing relation of our body to the steadiness of the world. If I go to the Grand Canyon, walk out onto an observation platform, and look down, at first I feel nausea. But, if I am able to continue looking, this feeling goes away in a few moments. What has happened? My whole being has filled the Grand Canyon, and I am actually held in a steady position from the side of the world. When, through this sense, the individual soul is held within the world soul, we feel steady and sure. What is around us holds us up. When we are unable to fill the space around us, unsteadiness results. If we walk out onto a stage to act or to speak to a group of people and experience stage fright, this is a disruption of the sense of balance; we have to stand there for a few moments, forget ourselves, and let our being fill the auditorium. While we are balanced by what is around us, we, through balance, also gain our own standpoint. Balance is the soul capacity to stand alone, to make something on one's own. This sense is the basis for true artistic activity. Artists must go so deeply into their own standpoint that it becomes universal. An artist expresses the world by letting his or her being fill the world. An exercise for strengthening this sense is to imagine walking into the lobby of a fifty-story skyscraper and taking the elevator to the observation deck. Imagine walking out onto the deck and looking straight down. If you feel nauseated, try to keep looking until the nausea ceases.

The sense of smell brings yet another quality of the soul experience of the body. In a way, smell is the opposite of balance. With balance, our being mingles with the Soul of the World. With smell we are pervaded by the Soul of the World; we take in something that is outside us. One cannot walk around an odor unless given advanced information of its existence. It comes into us; our entire being is permeated, and an odor can momentarily take away our consciousness.

The life sense concerns the sensation of how the body feels, whether good or ill, in pain, hungry, or thirsty. This sense is difficult to feel separately from the other senses. It is usually experienced only in its extremes, when we feel very good or not well, and is somewhat like a warning system. The interesting aspect of this sense concerns the capacity to sense when something is not as it should be, because in order to sense this, it is also necessary to sense the harmony of the body. If I wake up in the morning and feel lousy, that feeling relies on the sense of feeling good. What feeling good feels like is not here so much a memory as it is a sensing. The sensation of not feeling good, feeling pain, also includes psychological pain. Psychological pain is not in the mind, nor in the soul conceived as separate from the body.

Because of pain, we learn restraint and patience. Every feeling of discomfort cannot be immediately taken away; if pain is immediately removed or masked, our whole being cannot align. The life sense is the basis for conscience, the sensing that something is felt as pain. This sense is also the basis for compassion, for it is impossible to feel the pain of someone else unless one also senses it in one's own body. An exercise for strengthening the life sense is to imagine standing in a completely dark room, without any clothes, standing there naked. Imagine what you are feeling inside your body—not what you might be thinking or feeling, but the inner qualities of the body.

The outer senses do not provide the certainty of the body that is given with the inner senses, simply because the outer senses are more world-oriented and subject to manipulation. To be fully engaged in the world through the body, rather than to be an observer of the world from the place of the body, requires the on-going rhythmic harmony between inner and outer senses. If this rhythmical relation is unbalanced, confusion in sensing easily occurs.

The inner senses are crucial to accurate sensation and thus to the validity of imagination. One does not say, for example, "I can't believe my balance," but we often do not believe our eyes or our ears. One can, however, believe one's eyes and ears when the inner sensing circulates through the outer sensing—as when, for example, seeing is pervaded with a sense of touch. Paintings in an art museum often have an accompanying warning sign, "Do not touch the paintings," an indication that a true imagination, even if visual, is at the same time tactile. Similar signs are not needed at the entrance of a movie theater, for here the tactile sense is effectively disengaged from vision, and hence can be illusory.

When the inner senses are dimmed, the outer senses are also altered. Sensing cannot be divided simply into inner and outer, for, as we have said, the senses all work together. Dulling of the inner senses results in the outer senses becoming no more than physical structures through which we receive something like pictures of the outer world. The outer senses, in fact, are much more than physical apparatus for transmitting the outer world into representation.

When the outer senses function primarily as structures, the world is not experienced in its truly living, soul qualities. Hearing, for example, may seem to be no more than the reception by the physical apparatus of the ear of vibrations set up by a sounding body. When one hears in this manner, sound has no living, moving qualities. In order to really hear, it is also necessary for the body to be at that moment a completely sonorous being, actively reaching out to meet the sound that approaches. In a similar manner, seeing, when cut off from the total functioning which also involves the inner senses, results in the seeing of pictures of the world rather than a visual engagement of the whole body with the world.

The warmth sense, when not informed by the activity of the inner senses, becomes coarse, able to sense only extremes of physical temperature. The fact, for example, that colors are perceived not only by sight, but also through their warmth or coldness becomes only a metaphor without substance. The warmth of reds and the coolness of blues are not actual experiences any longer. Words are rightly mistrusted when only their cognitive meaning is comprehended and the life of the speaker is no longer a part of the word. Thinking becomes pure abstraction when its movement cannot be sensed in the world. And the individuality of another is reduced to a mere groundless idea when it cannot be sensed. The inner senses, the soul senses, make sensing a true activity of the body. If these senses are thwarted, the body functions more like an elaborate servomechanism.

Coming to Our Senses: the Necessity of Anger

Once we begin to respect the human body as a living unity of soul and spirit, and begin to realize that soul and spirit are not separate from body, we can begin the task of discovering the mode of love that can bring balance to the form of counter-creation. This mode of love is anger. A clue that anger may be a necessary form of love comes from the observation that anyone can have quite readily by silencing the onslaught of images from the outside for even a few minutes. What is often felt with a moment of true inner silence is a wave of anger.

When one begins to practice meditation for the first time, one is likely to encounter such an experience, which is certainly a surprise. The sensation is typically attributed to subconscious forces stemming from individual experiences of the past, and beginners are told that for progress in meditation to proceed, this feeling of anger must be overcome. I want to suggest, however, that the experience is valuable, for it is a direct sensing of the plight of the interior of the body cut off from functioning as soul forces. Through anger, we have access to the interior life of the suffering body, and our question becomes one of working with this sense of anger in a creative way.

Current psychologies may be all too quick to personalize all anger and see it as unexpressed emotion from the past. Certainly anger can stem from the past. But anger can also stem from the soul of the body being denied access to the time current from the future. The body, in its inner life, shut off from the world, is enraged. Since this anger is deep within the body, it is usually only dimly felt; but it needs to be experienced or it will work toward the detriment of bodily health. And, when one has enough presence of mind to feel anger in the presence of advertising, mindless television, senseless violence, manipulative entertainment, perhaps such anger should be listened to.

Anger clearly belongs to the realm of the body. It is how the body responds to something that is not right when there is no other way available to respond. Rightly stated, anger is an expression of the body as soul, a reaction to something sensed as wrong when there is no possibility of clearly seeing what is wrong and no clarity concerning what to do about it. What happens if the anger that arises when the world of counter-creation is momentarily stopped is not immediately dismissed? The anger can take over and become rage. In therapeutic treatment today, one is even encouraged to enter into rage, to go ahead and lose control in order to really feel the depth of one's anger. This encouragement becomes necessary when emotional life has been cut off, and I also encourage such rage toward the world of counter-creation. The intention here, however, is not simply to promote the egotism that comes when one feels the gratification of feeling one's emotions.

Anger easily turns into egotism when it turns into rage. Rage means that I no longer feel anger, but rather that I have become the anger; the ego has become completely taken over by the emotion. One becomes so self-centered that the world no longer exists. At such moments only anger exists. One then loses the sense of individuality. Nonetheless, when rage is felt in this way, a brief moment comes when we feel the powerlessness of ourselves within the anger. I am no longer in control, or, more accurately, the ego is no longer in control. One perhaps feels at such a moment, "I give up." Something like a gesture of throwing one's hands into the air in resignation arises as a feeling. But this giving up can signal the collapse of the ego and the possibility of the birth of the imaginal I. Anger thus becomes an educator of the ego, a way to the discover the primary functioning of the I, the body's activity of love, centered in the heart.

The experience of ourselves as an I can be looked at as a certain kind of sense experience. The human body is the body of Wisdom, the individualizing of Earth as Sophia. As long as the body is considered to be inert matter complexly arranged into systems of organs that function as a unified physiology, anything like soul, spirit, or mind will ultimately be abstractions—principles invented to attempt to account for how this complex material organization functions in ways that cannot be accounted for based on physical functions alone. Immediate experience suffices to bring into question a theory that divides the human being in this way. It suffices, that is, if what has been learned from the past about the body from biology, physiology, and medicine is not allowed to intrude as conceptual knowledge. Seeing soul and spirit as completely entwined with body is not a reduction, a way of getting rid of soul and spirit, but a way of giving attention to the whole.

The quality of the I is the sense experience of the body as love. The I, like other senses, has a particular function. The eye sees, the ear hears, the tongue tastes, the skin touches, the nose smells, and the heart loves. That is to say, the word *I* is a speaking of the heart, the way the heart speaks, its own sensing of everything inner and outer; the heart is the sense that synthesizes. When the heart is not in harmonious circulation through the realm of the inner and outer senses, individualizing the senses, keeping them active—or when the inner and outer senses are hindered in their activity so that they function as mere structures of transmission—then the heart also functions as a self-enclosed, self-sensing organ, the ego. Egotism is nothing more than love trying to function without a complete world in which to function.

The egotism of rage, then, can be seen as a functioning of the heart trying to do what it cannot do when blocked—love. Anger and rage are nothing more than the force of love that has been hindered. For this reason, anyone incapable of anger is also incapable of loving. Blessed be our anger, for it is the access to balancing the action of counter-creation. But, if our anger is taken to be only personal, or if we do not carefully work to distinguish between anger that is only personal and anger that senses something radically wrong in the world, then the resolution of anger will result in egotistical self-love rather than a self-love than can be turned toward the world. A further exploration of the heart's relation to the world can help in this discriminating act.

8

HEART AND
SOUL

WE DO NOT ordinarily think of the heart as a sense organ, except perhaps occasionally in a superficial and sentimental way. The heart of love has largely been replaced by the scientific view of the body. The now commonplace concept of the heart as a pump, however, is a serious misunderstanding, based on taking a partial view of reality to be the whole of reality. Medicine has found it useful to think of the heart as a pump, but then proceeds not only to forget that this is a metaphor but also to treat it as the only reality. Once this view is entrenched, there can be no possibility of understanding the heart as a sense organ; the mechanism metaphor opens the way for the heart to be treated only as a sentiment rather than a reality when not considered strictly as a physiological organ.

We can hear and feel our heart beating, but it is not in any sense experienced as a mechanical device. Rudolf Steiner warned of the problems of the mechanistic view of the heart:

> The heart is not a pump! I have often said this; it is rather an organ for sensing or registering the activity in the tissue fluid. The heart is moved by the circulation of the blood; it is not the pumping action of the heart that moves the blood. Just as the thermometer is nothing more than an instrument for registering the degree of heat or cold, so your heart is like an apparatus for registering what takes place in the circulation and what flows into this from the metabolic system. This is the golden rule we must heed if we wish

to understand the human being. In the belief that the heart is a pump driving the blood through the blood vessels, we can see how modern natural science reverses the truth. Anyone believing in this superstition about the heart ought to be consistent and believe it is warmer in the room because the thermometer has risen.[1]

In this more complete view, the heart is actually the organ that senses, in a synthesizing way, the inner activity of the senses. If we follow the line of thinking Steiner proposes, the further question arises: What accounts, then, for the circulation of the blood? The circulation of the blood, he replies, is an aspect of the body's participation in the world. In part, it concerns the forces of respiration, which have to do not only with breathing in and out, but with the senses as well, for the senses are part of this same circulation between inside and outside. We need, then, to picture the function of the heart in this sensing activity. Steiner once again gives a picture that can be the basis for further meditation:

Thus, we come to a remarkable picture, the picture of the human heart, with its interiorizing character, its synthesis of everything that works from the outside into our bodies. Outside in the world there is an analysis, a scattering of all that is gathered together in the heart. You come here to an important conception that might be expressed thus; you look out into the world, face the horizon and ask: What is in these outer surroundings? What works inward from the periphery? Where can I find in myself something that is akin to it? If I look into my own heart, I find, as it were, the inverted heaven, the polar opposite of the outside world. On the one hand you have the periphery, the point extended to infinity. On the other you have the heart, which is the infinite circle contracted to a point. The whole world is within our heart. . . . Picture to yourselves an individual standing looking on into the infinite expanse of the world, perhaps standing on a high hill, looking out and around. And suppose that the tiniest dwarf imaginable is put into the human heart. Try to realize that what the dwarf sees within the heart is the complete inverted image of the universe, contracted and synthesized.[2]

Here we have an image of the human heart in its relation to the world. The heart interiorizes the world. This interiorizing is the heart's action of recollection, of re-membering the world. All of what exists outside as a multiplicity of things, events, creatures, and beings is gathered together and synthesized as a point of concentration—which from the viewpoint of the body is the heart's sensing activity, and from the viewpoint of experiencing, that sensing is the I, the imaginal heart. We are continually forgetful of the fact that we experience a unified world. The heart re-members this unity, and in so doing also re-members the body in its unity of functioning.

Here, we also come upon a deeper and more profound sense of memory. While the independence from the past inaugurated through the explosion of the atomic bomb has destroyed the sense of continuity from the past, the task now is nonetheless to creatively re-member the past, based upon all that exists in the world from the past. Books, knowledge, art, music, architecture, objects— all of this exists in the world. The possibility and the task is to take in these artifacts as part of the sense world, now to be approached out of the time current from the future, through the heart. In recollecting the imaginal significance of all of the things of the world, we are actually moving within the unknown future.

Approaching this task from the heart means that one approaches everything in the world with the sense of not-knowing, as if discovering something for the first time. This nonacademic, noninstitutional approach to learning is available to everyone and can be a significant way of awakening the forces of the heart. We see this kind of learning going on quite frequently—people becoming deeply engaged in all sorts of fields of knowledge, not as specialists, but as researchers of the heart, individuals learning how to sense through the heart. Such study and learning is deeply moving because it is not carried out for self-aggrandizement—it usually does not result in gaining a degree or some other credential, but is a learning for the sake of the world, imagination as service.

Daily life can also be this same kind of ongoing research into the way of the heart, which consists of learning how to navigate in the time current from the future. Such a life of daily researching has no aim other than the researching itself. That is, one does not come to a result, or when one does it is entirely provisional and subject to change the next moment.

The Heart as Sense Organ

All of the sense organs, we have said, are both organs and capacities. The synthesizing action of the heart continuously creates a unity of the inner world and the outer world. Moments in which we perceive this unity are moments of the experience of beauty. Beauty is thus a consciousness of the heart.

The heart has always been connected with love due to this relation between bringing what seems to be separated into conjunction and the experience of such a conjoining as profound beauty. The invisible force of love within the heart is like a magnetic force that attracts the capacities of all of the other senses to a point of concentration, like the rhythmic contraction of the heart; the expansion of the heart follows, radiating into the world the unity of all that has been made in this split-second of mighty and intense focusing.

The heart thus might be spoken of as the organ of psychic attention. Becoming aware of this attentiveness of the heart involves becoming aware of the *act* of attention rather than of the *objects* of attention. Practicing such attentiveness involves, first of all, consciously shifting one's habitual sense of consciousness from the area of the head to the area between the heart and the solar plexus, and gradually becoming aware of the heart sense.

The practice brings about a new quality of perception in which sensing is no longer neutral, but carries inherently with it a sense of anguish or joy. The prevalence of anguish which is now experienced when attention is focused in this way is an indication that the world is every moment in great danger. The anguish one feels thus ought not to be taken as the pains of one's own personal life, any more than when we sense through the eyes or the ears we take what we sense as something only personal. When we see something in the world, we are confident that it is indeed the world that we are seeing. When we sense through the heart, we can likewise be confident that what is being sensed are qualities of the world.

The heart senses the world in such a manner that every sensing is also feeling, so educating this sense requires discerning the difference between personal emotion and world feeling. Egotism, which can be defined as being occupied with the contents of one's consciousness and the attendant emotion that a particular content may evoke, is the primary obstacle to discerning this difference. And even the *thought* of relinquishing egotism produces fear, because egotism seems to provide a secure foothold in the world.

While it is so that courage is required to practice sensing through the heart, this practice will not result in loss of the experience of oneself. Rather, a gradual shift away from personality and into individuality occurs, a movement from ego to the imaginal I. This is a movement from the I that acts in an illusory way, as if it knows who it is and what it is doing, to the I that is unfinished. This recognition of individuality is what separates the way of the heart from mysticism on the one hand, and from Eastern paths on the other; nonetheless the way of the heart honors the importance of both of these paths by attempting to incorporate their essential insights into a middle way. The middle way is a way into the world that does not strive to get beyond it, and consists in striving to become as attentive as possible to each moment through the medium of individuality. As has been said, the individualizing of the Earth can take place only through human individuality.

The contraction and expansion of the heart well defines the manner in which this sense organ senses the world. In the phase of contraction, the world as multiple appearances is concentrated to a point. In the phase of expansion, the heart radiates the soul sense of what is being experienced. This enhances the other senses. The ongoing infusion of the heart sense means that the senses actively engage the world, stream out into the world, individualizing what is being perceived; they do not simply receive what is there, as if the body were a recording apparatus. More accurately, there is a meeting with what comes to us from the world. In active, conscious sensing this meeting, like all true meeting, takes place in the space between my body and the object being perceived.

When we truly meet someone, we have to forget ourselves a bit, put ourselves forward, go out beyond ourselves, which is an active, bodily experience. To meet the world in such a way that the world shifts from an "it" to a "thou" in a moment of creative, imaginal perception, similarly requires presence to the radiating quality of the heart sense. When the sensing of the heart is consciously, actively engaged, the model of perception shifts from one of transmission and reception to one of meeting. Conscious sensing here does not imply a mental awareness of what is happening as we sense the world. When the focus centers in the region of the heart, a more subtle awareness than the mental occurs, an awareness that can be described as a striving of the heart.

The heart strives. When we are in the presence of another person, it is quite possible to have something go back and forth between myself and that person without a meeting taking place. Only when the heart is engaged in the relationship is meeting possible. It is the same in our relationships with the world. Striving, or a willing of the heart, is like the sacrifice of the ego, its releasing of its own experience of itself in order to experience the life of the world. Looking at an object and immediately cataloging what that object is, only to pass on to the next object or event, filling our day with passing by the world as it appears in front of us, is immensely different from striving to meet what appears to us.

Such striving has two effects. It invites the things and events of the world to show themselves in their active soul qualities, and it gradually transmutes the body from its object-like passivity into a presence radiating out into the world. When we see a person who loves, we see his or her radiance, an actual quality of the body. Thus, we are not speaking here of something fantastic, and need not use terms such as the "light body" or the "astral body." Our vocabulary for the love of the heart attempts to describe what can be present for anyone through attentiveness. The heart sense develops through attempting to meet the world, through developing the capacity of attentiveness to attention itself, and through taking a stance toward the world that does not attempt to hold on to any experience, that is to say, one that avoids being bribed by the comfort of knowledge possessed.

When one feels the life of the world through the heart, the tendency is very strong to fall into emotional response, in order to break the tension experienced in the moment of meeting. When this at-tension is broken, one may then go about looking for special instances that produce mere emotion, which can be easily had in the realm of counter-creation. Thus, learning to stay with the tension of the sensing heart is required. The aim is not catharsis, but to live with and in the intent of the heart, to live a transforming life without ever seeking an imagined end to the transformation.

Here, we come to the essential relation between the heart and thinking. Heart is not opposed to thinking, and when they are separated and the forces of the heart are developed outside of the activity of thinking, the result is the production of magic. Magic is a technology of the heart, utilizing the heart to bring about specific and desired effects in oneself and in the world. We need to find, instead, an approach that does not gravitate between abstract ideas on the one hand, and a technology of the heart that seeks transformation experiences on the other.

For example, once the counter-creating world is seen through, one quite rightly wishes to do something about it. If, however, development of the heart is taken as the means for bringing change into the world rather than as a needed force of balancing that occurs right in the midst of counter-creation, then heart will be looked to as a magical means of eradicating what one finds reprehensible. A great deal of depth psychology and "New Age" practices tend toward this direction. Thus, in such movements we find attempts to develop various technologies of the heart—dream work, ritual work, meditation work, inner imagination work—but what is decidedly lacking is imaginal work with the world as it presents itself.

Heart sensing is also heart thinking in the way we are here seeking to develop an imagination of the heart. What is necessary in order to keep these two together is to not confuse our thought with the activity of thinking. Thought is always from the past—using past concepts to think about present things. Thought is in us, but thinking is in the world—the world as Wisdom, as Sophia—and thus is it necessary to be engaged bodily with the world to be in the activity of thinking. But, the only access to bodily participation in the world—that is, the only way to be *in* it instead of having it before us—is through the heart. Here, *in* the world, the sense of thinking is different than what it is when the world is seen as "out there." The ego thinks from the past; but when heart senses the world, the world thinks through the I. For the heart, love and thinking are the same thing.

Heart and Action

Approaching the question of how the heart acts in the world means also re-imagining the will. We usually think of action as stemming from an idea. Will is applied to an idea to bring about an action in the world. This sequence describes the calculative will, what Heidegger calls the tyranny of calculative thought. The will of the brain has become the citadel of the forces of counter-creation. The will of the brain and the will of the heart are quite different, and to get at this difference we need only to reinstate the mysteriousness of will in its connection with the body. For example, how is it possible for an individual to do an act as simple as moving the arm? If I have the thought, I am going to move my arm, how does that thought ever result in movement? Does the thought "push" the material, physical body? How that thought moves into the physiology of the muscles can never be understood because will does not move from the brain into the movement of the muscles. That explanation of will is no more than a theory.

A person whose capacity of consciousness is dimmed, for example, through hypnotism, may respond to what is suggested without the intervention of thinking about it before carrying out the act. The body itself responds to the suggestion and comes under the sway of another who speaks directly to the body. Seeing someone act under the force of suggestion, one cannot help but be impressed with the mechanical nature of the action. In ordinary life, what is usually termed will is no more than carrying out similar suggestions spoken to the body from our own interior voice. Thus, what we speak of as will is more like the response of an automaton in which we are both the voice in control and the responding automaton. This mode of action is so habitual that it looks "real," that is, the automatic character is scarcely perceptible. Further, such automatic action of the will requires that the active heart not be included in the circuit.

The will of the heart does not operate in this manner. What the heart wills does not bring about a direct result. Here, one does not will that this or that will happen. Suppose a person who is greatly confused asks for my advice and help. If I make a specific suggestion concerning what to do, the strong possibility is that the individual will respond by taking up the suggestion, not directly, as in hypnosis, but by interiorizing what was heard, which then becomes the inner voice that speaks directly to that person's body. The body responds by carrying out the suggested action.

If we look at our lives as objectively as possible, we can see that much of what we do and call actions of our will are no more than automatic responses. Suppose, however, that when this individual asks for suggestions concerning what to do, I do not give such suggestions; instead I sense what is being said in the region of the heart and, from that sensing, imagine an unknown future for that individual in which his or her question leads to a seeking of destiny. I do not have a picture of the actual destiny of the person, for that is something I cannot know. I do wish, with my heart, that the person's questions lead to a capacity to sense the time current from the future, and that he or she can follow that current into the unknowing.

Such a heartfelt desire for the destiny of another works back from the future and can affect the actions of a person, though in entirely unknown ways, and in ways that have not controlled the actions of the person. The will of the heart seeks to help without having a specific idea of what, for a particular individual, constitutes the help needed. The heart can will the good of the person, and this will have an effect on the actions of the person without interfering with that individual's freedom.

Thus, in willing through the heart, I do not become concerned with how I can bring about a particular result that I may want to happen. A particular situation leads me to speak in a manner that proceeds out of the place of the heart, seeing through love. It leads me to listen carefully to the other person, seeking to hear how this particular situation being described contains a direction toward the unknown future. In refraining from responding according to what I think or what I know, or from my own past experience, which in any case does not relate to the individuality of the other person, we together hold the question in such a manner that the particular situation can be seen as a possibility of creating through the heart.

Heart and Obsession

A particular difficulty encountered in working to open the heart center is finding a way through the hazard of obsession. Entering the domain of the heart means no longer relying on the ordinary empirical ego, our assumed sense of who we are that comes from what we have been taught and given by others, our memories, our past experiences, and habitual concepts. As living from the past drops away, we will feel empty. The feeling of emptiness can quickly be invaded by fear. Obsession consists either of compulsive thoughts or of compulsive acts that attempt to rid one of fear.

A mother might fear, for example, that her anger could lead her to kill her children; so she becomes afraid to be left alone with them. A person might go through elaborate, repetitive rituals every night, locking all the doors and then proceeding to check fifty times to see if all the doors are locked. These more clinical sorts of obsession are not so common these days. The psychiatrist, Arthur Guirdham, speaking of clinical obsession, indicates that "at the present time it expresses itself in a clandestine way with greater effect and inflicts more mortal wounds in the form of coronary disease and the cardiovascular catastrophes that follow hypertension."[3]

He thus establishes a link between heart and obsession. In the present time, obsession, besides expressing itself in heart ailments of a physical nature, also appears in the uncontrollable, impulsive longings of the heart. How does fear enter into this kind of obsession?

Throughout this work, I have alluded to the fact that in the extraordinary complexity of the present world, it is no longer simple to say what is good and what is evil. Further, evil is not to be avoided nor fought against. We must learn to navigate through the mixture of good and evil if the heart is to remain open. Obsession is a danger only when strong heart emotions take place in the absence of the sense of the I. In other words, when ego defenses are let down and heart emotion is felt, it must never be forgotten that love is for the sake of the world, and the world must be included.

The phenomenon of obsession in the modern world is quite pervasive. Love between individuals these days often results in obsession. Much of the recovery movement is concerned with how to avoid obsession. The notion is that when a person who did not receive proper love as a child falls in love as an adult, he or she is actually seeking the love that was never received as a child. In an adult relationship, this absence of proper love in one's history means that if anything at all seems to threaten the relationship, fear will arise, causing a person to do all sorts of destructive things to try to keep the partner as a possession.

When two people with a history of an absence of love in childhood get together, which is usually the case, then there is the mutual destructiveness of codependency. Codependency means that one person relies on being treated badly by the other person and vice versa, but the whole thing is disguised as obsessive love. The work suggested is to learn to love oneself, discover the inner child, and love that child and grow it up, because one can never receive the love that was never received as a child.

I do not wish to speak against this way of approaching the difficulty of obsession, but rather to suggest that the phenomenon is far more pervasive than realized thus far, and that it may not be due only to what has happened to us as children. The phenomenon of obsessiveness in love is also related to the old sense of the ego breaking down. In part, I want to suggest that the force of love is stronger in the world than it has ever been in human history, but we do not yet see that the reason for this gift of love is for love to be oriented toward the regeneration of the Soul of the World.

But, evil is also stronger in the world than it has ever been in human history. Thus, opening the heart requires the capacity to work with fear as well as with love. When a person becomes obsessed with another person, the obsessiveness is not about love, but about fear. Someone who becomes obsessed in love is also someone with an open heart, subject to imagining all sorts of realities. Not all obsession can be traced back to what one did not receive as a child. When a loved one does not act as one expects—that is, when the loved one acts out of true individuality which cannot be perceived unless the other person also senses his or her own individuality—fear enters. In many instances, this fear turns into cruelty. The obsession that results, with all of the repetitive, uncreative acts—like calling the person every five minutes, following the person home, watching his or her home—is actually a ritual act that functions to protect one from sheer panic. Seen in this way, the work to be done involves the development of the sense of individuality in the ways that have been suggested thus far. That is, the work is not perhaps to strengthen our ego in order to be in control of ourself, but to decide to work on becoming a creative being who creates through love. The development of true individual love, which also encompasses the world, means that the very meaning of love relationships between individuals needs re-visioning in light of the Soul of the World.

9

SOULFUL
RELATIONSHIPS

IN THIS TIME, relationships of an intimate nature are becoming more and more difficult. Here, the future indeed
looks bleak. In twenty-five years of practicing as a psychotherapist,
I have never worked with a single person who did not give this
problem a central place. I have tried to work archetypally, attempting to get a sense of what god, goddess, daimon, or spirit might be
trying to get attention. I have worked with retrieving the inner
child, with interpersonal dynamics, with helping individuals to
learn to focus more on their own soul. I have looked at relating
more as an imaginal reality than a literal interaction, tried to convince people that they should not look to another person to be the
carrier of all that one needs, encouraged more open expression
between couples, seen people individually and with their partners,
alternated single sessions and couple sessions. I have watched in
amazement, seeing that always some other factor is involved. In
many instances relationships changed, but in no instance did relating ever cease to be a struggle.

I know what people are looking for; it is usually foreshadowed
there at the outset of coming together—to truly know the individuality of another, and to be known by another in one's true
individuality. But what is given as a gift at the outset cannot be
retained. It is a strange fact indeed, that the beginning of a relationship is where we seem to know each other best, and all that
follows seems to be watching this slip away.

The Illusion of Intimacy

Relationships of an individual nature cannot be separated from the field of our relationships with others in the world. It is impossible to conceive of a safe haven of intimacy in a world fraught by strife and disharmony. Yet, do we not expect exactly this state of affairs? A division between the individual soul and the world first of all works to divide our connections with others in the world from our intimate connection with a specific individual. Because of this division, marriage is in a state of crisis; for marriage unites two individuals, not only to each other, but equally to the community and the world.

What now prevails in the world is brutality of one person toward another, one group toward another, one community toward another, one nation toward another. Given this situation, what is most likely to happen between two individuals is the attempt to dissolve into each other as a way to seek respite from the cruelty of the world. What one discovers instead is suffocation, necessitating its own sort of cruelty, and destroying the possibility that the individual relationship can become a force radiating into the wider world.

A certain hopelessness exists in this domain, but a hopelessness that few are ready to acknowledge. I see the refusal to give in to hopelessness as true hope that a balance can be found that will bring a new consciousness from the future into getting along together. Once again, entry into new, unknown modes of experience is not easy and requires the unity of the I with the world.

I must preface what is to follow with a bit of a warning. Much of what is to be said seems, on the surface, to be at odds with practically everything that modern psychology and psychotherapy have to say about relationships. I do not intend to be at odds, but modern psychology, including psychologies oriented toward soul, have not recognized the importance of the Soul of the World. The meaning of relationships changes considerably when this factor is taken into account.

First, some of our most tightly held illusions concerning intimacy need to be faced. The first illusion is that it is really possible to encounter, in a direct manner, the soul and spirit of another person. The presence of the ego dimension of consciousness makes such a direct encounter impossible. We are each "screened" from the other. We do not encounter what another person thinks or feels in relationships, but rather what that person thinks and feels about us, and vice versa. At first, that encounter can be exciting, for in finding out about the other person we are in fact finding out about ourselves, even though it seems as if we are learning about the other person.

As time continues, however, we also find out a lot about ourselves that is distinctly unpleasant; and, since that knowledge is coming from someone else, it is far easier to say that the unpleasantries really belong to the other person, and were hidden at first because we really did not know him or her. Depth psychology calls all of this projection. It is not projection at all, but is due to the fact that the ego is like a mirror, in the presence of which we can see only ourselves. The only time this mirror is not there is when we are sleeping together, and I do not mean making love. When we are asleep, then my partner and I are truly together in soul and spirit. The rest of the time, we are adjusting to the presence of ourselves seen through each other, spending a great deal of time with our double.

Closely connected with the illusion that intimacy means participating in the soul and spirit life of another person is the feeling that such participation should, if not available, be sought with all of one's effort. One feels a terrible need to make connection with the soul of another, not realizing that it is one's own soul that is being sought. In fact, when an individual does have direct access to the soul and spirit of another person, it is an indication of a psychological illness; it indicates that the person seeking such connection wants power over the other person, and it indicates that the person yielding to such a direct connection does not live a fully conscious waking life and is subject to being invaded by the partner.

To suggest that what each of us seeks in relationship is in fact founded in illusion is to speak only from the viewpoint of the ordinary waking consciousness of daily life. Here the mysteries of soul and spirit are still partly veiled; that is, they are available only to fully awake consciousness. A long development of the conscious imaginal I will be required before soul and spirit can be expressed directly. The fact that we cannot really know the soul and spirit of another person, however, is exactly what love is about, for love means to establish an intimate relationship with the not-known.

We are each alone in the world, completely separated from others. A healthy relationship starts from this basis and does not attempt to resolve this unbridgeable gap in a direct way. Whenever it does try to do so, something from the past is trying to be enacted —for example, the union one had or never had with one's parents—and what is thus felt as intimacy is actually divisiveness. This gap is bridged in the best possible way through meeting the other person, not soul to soul, but through coming together in the place of the World Soul as mediator. If the world can be experienced as soul-filled, then a meeting of individuals can take place in soul.

Being Carried by Love

Much that is today spoken of as love between people does not have to do with creating love, but with being carried by love. Ordinary language carries this sense of expecting and hoping to be carried by love. We say, love will get us through; I don't know what to do, but love will find a way; as long as we are together, everything will work out. But, as we know, love does not always carry us. When it does not, the institution of marriage is expected to carry us until love reappears. Now, however, we are entering a time, an epoch, in which love must be created; and it must be created in relation not only one to another, but also in relation with the world. If we do not learn to do this creating work, the institution of marriage will not help, for there will be nothing for it to contain.

Depth psychology has helped show us the particular ways that we are carried by love, and to make us more conscious that this is the case. Depth psychology, however, has not been so helpful in indicating how to move away from being carried by the force of love to creating the force of love that involves the world. We need only to look at the founding myths of the two great depth psychologies, the psychology of Freud and that of Jung, to see why they can help make us more conscious, but not more conscious that relationships involve the world. Freud's psychology places the Oedipus myth at the center of its sense of soul, so let us begin with this myth.

Laius, the king of Thebes, and his wife Jocasta had no children, and Laius feared that they would be given none. He consulted the oracle at Delphi to ask whether they might have a son. The answer received was that a son would be born to them, but that this son would kill his father. After Oedipus was born, Laius began to be apprehensive, fearing the fulfillment of the prophecy. He took Oedipus, pierced his feet, and abandoned him in the wilderness. Oedipus was found by a shepherd, who took him to Corinth, where he grew up in the house of a king. When he was grown, he heard about the oracle, but nonetheless left Corinth in search of his home. Along the way he came across his real father, whom he did not recognize, and killed him. He then came to Thebes.

Thebes was under the siege of the Sphinx, and the only way to defeat this monster was to solve the riddle of the Sphinx. If anyone solved this riddle, the Sphinx would kill herself. The riddle is, "What walks on four legs in the morning, on two legs at mid-day, and on three legs at evening?" Oedipus was able to answer this riddle, that it is man. Answering the riddle required that one have a true understanding of the human being, which Oedipus had. Because he answered this riddle, the Sphinx had to kill herself, which saved Thebes, for this monster had brought death to many there. Oedipus was made king and received the hand of the queen, who was his mother. He also did not recognize her. Because he killed his father and married his mother, immeasurable suffering was brought upon the land—famine, disease, and pestilence. When Oedipus learned of what he had done and the result, he blinded himself.

This story is one image of relationships when they are unconsciously formed from something out of the past rather than from movement into an unknown future. It is a picture of what occurs when there is no consciousness of a mediating factor in relating. It also says that relating to another through the blood is a destructive form of relationship. The question here, though, is not really one of the incest taboo. At the time Sophocles wrote this play, many relationships were still in fact relationships of the blood. What we now speak of as love between individuals did not exist. Love between individuals who meet as strangers began just a little over seven hundred years ago. Prior to that, love was something that lived strongly in the blood, and people came together out of blood relationships. One married someone who lived in the same continuity of time, someone from the same tribe, clan, or family.

The question here concerns what soul quality was being expressed through relationships of the blood, and it is the quality of memory. Relating, when it occurred through blood lines, meant that when two people came together to form a bond, the factor that united them was the memory of all the past that lived in the blood. This was not just the past of the two people involved. This memory also extended across generations, so that in uniting one with another, the true bond was with all of the past. For a long time, this memory of the blood was expressed through the custom that children received the same name as the parent—someone who was John the fifth still experienced what John the first experienced of the world. This bond with the past was an actual experience. Through relationships of the blood, people still lived in the realities that were lived by former generations. Here we see that in any relationship, a third is involved; it is never just what goes on between two people. In former times, memory intervened as the third in relationships. For our own time, the question of the third becomes central: What is the third through which two people can come into relationship in the present world? The blood is no longer involved.

The Oedipus myth is a picture of the end of relationships occurring through the medium of memory carried in the blood. When Oedipus meets the queen of Thebes, he does not recognize her as his mother. We look at that and say he could not have recognized her because he had not seen her since he was an infant. But the memory of the blood at one time was stronger than the forgetfulness of past perception. If blood memory had still been active, Oedipus would have felt a connection of familiarity to his mother. He would have instinctively felt that this connection was too close, that such a marriage violated even the laws of blood relationships. He instead perceived her as a stranger. Thus, we have a picture of two people brought together by the force of the blood, without the recognition of the blood connection.

But, it is also a long distance from ancient Greece to modern psychoanalysis—so what so attracted Freud to this myth? Presently, a great deal of controversy surrounds this question. Until recently, the answer would have been this: Freud recognized that while relating through the blood was no longer a reality, and had not been for centuries, nevertheless, the form of relationships through the blood had been transferred to the soul realm. Thus, unconsciously, one seeks to marry someone who is like his mother or someone who is like her father (the Electra complex), and looks toward the other parent with hatred. What previously existed as actual fact had now become incorporated in the soul as a primary longing of the soul. Freud, from this point of view, was involved in bringing to an end a form of relating that can no longer work now that the task is to find a way to love that is not bounded by the past. Analysis roots out the unconscious fantasy, making one freer in his or her way of relating. But, this freedom is not the freedom to create love; it is the freedom to strengthen the ego, to try to make sure that one takes care of oneself first in relationship.

There is now a whole other school of thought concerning Freud's work. This school suggests that the destructiveness of love through blood relationship was not ever brought to an end, and that literal incest, literal reenactment of versions of the Oedipus story, is responsible for a large number of psychological difficulties. It is quite possible that both readings are correct. Whether the myth is literally enacted or works more as a soul factor, the result is always destructiveness. We no longer relate to someone with whom there is a connection in time, indirectly through generations; and when relating takes place as if this kind of connection still exists, destructiveness results.

Now we have to find how to relate to someone who stands next to us in space, someone encountered as a stranger. The crucial factor to be looked at in the present, however, is the question of the third. Today people who come into relationship based upon what they experienced in their own family life, hoping to carry on this pattern in the present, perhaps improving it because the way their family did it was flawed, are bound to find this impossible. Even short-term memory can no longer serve as the connecting medium through which people relate. We have become too conscious for that. Yet we all still start out relationship trying to do it the way that our parents did it, even when we resolve that this will not be the case. No matter what the intention, relating through the ego knows no other way than what it is given through the past.

Jung's psychology is based also on a love story, the Eros and Psyche myth. This myth tells another way in which we are carried by love, but it also gives very little in the way of help to get free of this situation.

While Jung spoke a great deal about Eros and about Psyche individually, it is James Hillman who located the myth as lying at the heart of depth and archetypal psychology. The tale is told in the *Metamorphosis* of Apuleius. The mortal Psyche is born to a king and queen. She is not the only offspring, but has two beautiful sisters. Psyche's beauty outshines their beauty, and indeed that of every other mortal woman. She is so beautiful that people cease paying homage to Venus, and instead give divine honor to Psyche. Venus, outraged, demands that her son Eros bring it about that a man of the worst sort should fall in love with Psyche.

While Psyche was most beautiful, she received no suitors. Her father consulted the oracle of Apollo to see what to do. He was instructed to leave Psyche abandoned on a mountain, where an immortal would come to be her husband. Rather than finding an unsavory character for her, Eros comes and makes her his own bride, but he remains always in the dark. Eventually, Psyche is allowed to arrange a visit with her two sisters so that they will know that she has not perished. When they see the riches surrounding her, they become infected with envy, and plot against her. They convince her that her husband is a huge snake and help her devise a plan to see him; she is to hide a lamp in the bedchamber, and remove the veil from the lamp when he is in bed.

When Eros is sleeping, Psyche removes the lamp from the dark and sees him. He is beautiful. A drop of oil from the lamp falls on Eros and wakes him, and he flees.

Psyche is then put through a series of trials by Venus. She must separate a pile of mixed seeds, capture a handful of fleece, retrieve a pitcher of water from a high mountain spring, and journey to the

Underworld to capture some of Persephone's beauty in a small box for Venus. When Psyche opens the box to use some of the beauty for herself, it contains not beauty but rather sleep. Eros revives her from her depth of sleep and then pleads his case before Jupiter, who grants his wish to marry Psyche. They have an offspring, Joy. Venus is restored to honor.

This story is another image of intimate relationships, one which makes the medium of psychic fantasy the third through which two individuals meet. It is not memory that holds people together, says this myth, but fantasy, imagination. Eros (love) remains dark and invisible to the mortal Psyche (soul). Psyche suffers. And Eros without Psyche is also left in burning pain. Through the intervention of envy, imagination is stimulated, and Psyche begins to fantasize. In our relationships, this indicates that love awakens the psyche, and psyche cools the burning of love. We may think that we are in love, but we really do not see the person we think we love. We have a love fantasy, and believe that fantasy refers directly to the person. We fall in love with love, not with another person.

A long, tortuous series of trials follows. It is as if we have to begin in the realm of fantasy and then differentiate one fantasy from another and enact one myth after another without end, or until we realize that we are always within myth. With this mythic imagination, relationships really do not have much to do with the love of one person for another. What we call love is no more than the necessary condition for the development of psychic interiority. Psychic interiority, here, however means realizing that it is the gods that create personality; and further, these gods, in archetypal psychology, are always pictured in images from the past—primarily as the Greek gods of Western civilization.

Two aspects of the Jungian approach to relationships need to be considered. The first is that here again we come to a stance, similar to that of Freud, that a third is always involved in a relationship; it is never, never, just you and me. The second aspect to consider is the relative impotence of fantasy as the medium of relationship; in Jung's understanding, we are being carried by love, one psychic enactment of myth after another. The problem here, as we have seen, is that unless the world can be included in the activity of imagination, a way to the future cannot be found.

Memory cannot initiate a love that is creative, and fantasy cannot initiate a love that is creative. What brings people together in the first place, that may be due to something out of the past. And what attracts one person to another, that may be due to the fantasies involved. The possibility of relating at all is closely involved with these things. But the possibility of individual love that can create something in the world, that comes from the future. Here a different third is involved: one that does not carry us in love, but makes possible love as a creative force for which we are responsible. The third here is not blood memory or psychic fantasy but the Soul of the World, Sophia—whose self-unfolding is of one piece with the individuation of our own souls.

We meet through the world and the world benefits from our relationship, which makes that relationship more than an initiation into memory and more than an initiation into mythic psychologizing. Care of the soul then means not care of memory or care of imagination, but care of the world—active remembering of the presence of the world, and fully conscious imagining through which Earth is perceived as a living being. Trying to find love by turning away from the world, seeking love without the world, as if it involved just you and me, would keep this third in obscurity. And when the world is not included as integral to relating, it begins to appear so harsh and strife-filled that retreat into the illusion of one-to-one relating is stimulated.

Psychic interiority is a must, but it is not enough because we also belong to the world, and thus the world cannot be left out without interiority being captured by egotism, now turned into psychic egotism. Rather than try to find ways around the ego, do we not need to find a way through the ego into imaginal I consciousness? If this is possible, then psyche and world can cohere—not one without the other. The I is the pivot point between soul and World Soul.

Relating through the World

We are now ready to see how intimacy becomes quite different when the connecting third is seen to be the Soul of the World than when it is either memory or fantasy. As we become accustomed to imagining relationships as a triad rather than a dyad, the question that arises is how to actually picture this triadic relationship in its operation. Further, how are we to picture this operation with respect to its meaning for what transpires in an intimate relationship? Working with these questions takes us not only into a new understanding of relationships, but also into deeper understanding of Sophia.

Goethe came close to an understanding of Sophia. He was an astute observer of the world through the capacity of imagination. His scientific studies of color, plants, and animals provide an imagination of the world that is not based on detached observation, experiment, and theory, but on a fully conscious imaginative participation. For him, archetypal imagination was a world phenomenon. He has this to say concerning self-knowledge: "I have always looked with suspicion on the grandiloquent injunction: Know Thyself. It seems to me a ruse on the part of priests secretly in league with one another for the purpose of confusing man with unattainable demands, of leading him away from activity directed toward the outside world to a false inner contemplation. Man knows but himself insofar as he knows the world, for he sees the world but in himself, and himself in it alone." We might further this observation by saying that one knows another only insofar as one knows the world.

Sophia, the Soul of the World, is the world as psychic reflection. Earth first of all reflects the whole cosmos—the Moon and the Sun, the planets, and all of the stars. Reflection here means imagination and not mere mirroring. The body of Earth is Wisdom, the embodied imagination of the totality of the cosmos. Every flower here is a reflection of a star in the heavens, an imagination of the heavens. Every animal here is a living imagination of the constellations, some of which even bear the names of animals. Likewise, the metals of the Earth each are an imagining of a planet—gold is the Sun, silver is the Moon, iron is Mars, copper is Venus, and all the rest. The Wisdom of the cosmos is reflected as the multiplicity of every appearing thing in the world.

Reflection is also an attribute, a quality of the individual soul life of human beings. Reflection that has become conscious of itself as reflection is what we call individual imagination. The whole of Earth as an imagination of the cosmos is also repeated in the structure and functioning of the human being. And the inner Earth is reflected as the interiority of the human being; the psyche of the human being as something deep inside is the imagination of the interior of the Earth, necessary to the individualizing of the Soul of the World.

The breadth and depth of Sophia is all-encompassing, and places us on the verge of losing the capacity to stay with the subject at hand. Central to consideration of relating out of the time current from the future is the close connection to be found between Sophia as Soul of the World and woman. In the triad woman–world–man, a certain priority of woman emerges due to imagining the World Soul as Sophia. I am here not speaking of matriarchy versus patriarchy. Nor does priority signify superiority. I also cannot use the word *feminine* because the feminine is either an abstract concept or a strictly invisible reality. Earth is neither of these. Nor am I suggesting a feminist stance. These conceptual modes belong to or are reactions to the past. I am not reacting to the past but envisioning a future.

In considering new forms of intimate relationship that are needed to bring balance to being carried by love, an imagination of the womanly nature of Sophia and her relation to women may put us on a truly different track. This kind of imagination can be developed without making women into goddesses on the one hand, and without reducing Sophia to mortal women on the other. A capacity to remain with a sense of resemblance, of likenesses and similarities, is required to follow this tightrope without stumbling into deification of mortals or mortification of the goddesses.

Intimacy and the World Soul

What then does relating through the womanly, and imagining the womanly through Sophia imply? What specific qualities of intimacy are involved? Here, Sophia herself is our guide; she speaks concerning things that every woman knows but may not have the language to speak. Let us listen to what Sophia has said about herself and the world, about who she is and what she does, in those instances that have particular relevance for intimate relating. The aim of our listening is not to recover an archetype, or to become more familiar with the "Eternal Feminine," but rather to learn how to approach relationship from the viewpoint of the womanly.

> *Does not wisdom call,*
>> *does not understanding raise her voice?*
> *On the heights beside the way,*
>> *in the paths she takes her stand;*
>> *beside the gates in front of the town,*
>> *at the entrance of the portals she cries aloud:*
> *"To you, O men, I call,*
>> *and my cry is to the sons of men.*

O simple ones, learn prudence;
O foolish men, pay attention.
Hear, for I will speak noble things,
and from my lips will come what is right;
for my mouth will utter truth;
wickedness is an abomination to my lips.
All the words of my mouth are righteous;
there is nothing twisted or crooked in them.
They are all straight to him who understands
and right to those who find knowledge.
Take my instruction instead of silver,
and knowledge rather than choice gold;
for wisdom is better than jewels,
and all that you may desire cannot compare with her.
I, wisdom dwell in prudence,
and I find knowledge and discretion.
By me kings reign
and nobles govern the earth.
I love those who love me,
and those who seek me diligently find me."

(Proverbs 8:1–17)

With respect to relating, what is here revealed about this womanly quality is that relationship belongs to the realm of public life. Sophia appears at the gates of the city. When the World Soul is the third of relationship, then intimacy is public, not private. Desire, passion, and their expression may be private, something that needs to take place behind closed doors; but intimacy is worldly and practical, a matter of prudence. Men enter the marketplace to make money; but that is not practical wisdom, not the practice of wisdom, for it uses the world rather than seeking communion with it. When Earth is considered as resource rather than source, love is actually diminished. Using the world uses up love, for Earth is love. This is not to say that the world is not to be seen as making things available; but these things are gifts and whatever is taken from her must be returned in some form. She says, "I love those who love me." In loving the world, we find ourselves loving one another. Then, we may not need to make a project out of remaining close, for the world is always at hand.

As long as intimacy is confused with desire and passion, with the expression of personal feelings, with sex, with being close to another person without realizing the necessity of the third of the world, all of the problems of the past carried in memory, and all of the fantasies that erotic love inspires will dominate and make relationships difficult—and in the future, even more difficult than they now are. Men and women need to be together in the world, working together, sharing a common interest, an interest that goes beyond themselves, an interest in the future of the world. This common interest does not necessarily mean taking up a cause together, finding joint employment in ecology.

Knowledge has been removed from the world, made into abstractions and put into the educational institutions; this, when Wisdom, Sophia, the Earth, says that she is knowledge. So, working together in the world is also a matter of re-education, of learning through the world, of developing the capacity to find out what is needed in the moment in the particular situations, of not knowing in advance what to do. When partners put themselves into this kind of not-knowing relationship with the world, they also find themselves close to each other. Marriages usually start out this way, couples working together, not knowing how they are going to do it; but then marriages tend to slide into ease and comfort, because the effort is too self-oriented.

The ability to find out what is needed in the moment is also a matter of the immediacy of perception. Sophia is Wisdom, and wisdom lives deep in the body and flows into the senses. We do not have to think about how to move our arms or legs, or consider how to make our heart beat. Nor do we have to figure out how to make the eye see, the ear hear. Sophia is the content, process, and object of perception—she is in the body and in the world. A wise sage says:

> Listen my children, to a father's instruction:
>> pay attention, and learn what clear perception is.
> What I am commending to you is sound doctrine;
>> do not discard my teaching. . . .
> Acquire Sophia, acquire perception;
> Never forget her, never deviate from my words.
> Do not desert her, she will keep you safe,
>> love her, she will watch over you.
>
> (Proverbs 4:1–2, 5–6)

Perception is the body's immediate knowing of things in their unity through the unity of the senses. The passage does not speak of a singular mode of perception, such as visual or auditory or tactile. Perception is a cognitive act of the body, knowing that is at the same time feeling. It is not knowing at a distance, but intimate knowledge; it is not the same as instinct because it contains consciousness. It is not abstract knowing or knowing something in a general way, but is specific, particular, intuitive, sensitive apprehension of things in their qualities, imaginative knowing.

The key phrase in the passage, "Acquire Sophia, acquire perception," also gives the key to forming relationships in a new and different way. We can read the passage as saying that if you acquire Sophia, then you acquire perception, and if you acquire perception,

then you acquire Sophia. The implication is that what we ordinarily think of as perception is not perception at all; what we ordinarily
call perception is no more than a cognitive knowing of things that
we already know in advance, not a meeting. With perception as
Sophia, everything is seen as a cipher, an emblem, a signature, a
glyph, an outward gesture revealing the inward Soul of the World
coming into being. If we perceive things merely as objects, we miss
the soul quality of all things of the world.

Perception is not the inward reception of something that is
already formed, already finished; it cannot be, because the body is
living, changing, becoming, not already finished. Perception is thus
a genesis rather than a conclusion; it is the opening into the world
as becoming. Relationship as a triad with the world as the third,
then, is not something that one has or even something that one is
in, but a coming-to-be together. A relationship is always a genesis, an advent, an opening, something always at its beginning rather
than an event.

Further, since Sophia is acquired, and perception is acquired,
this says something about soul. Soul is not an entity, not even an
entity of an immaterial nature. Acquired, here, does not mean something to be had as a possession; to acquire Sophia means to acquire
a capacity, not an object. Relating with another is thus an active
capacity, like developing a new organ of perception, the capacity to
perceive through the heart, with the world at the center.

In relating through the medium of the world, we are continually involved in a research into ourselves and into the world.
Constant adjustments of knowing go on; the instant we think our
relationship is just right, some unknown factor enters which
changes the whole thing. These unknowns do not involve simply
discovering more of the other person that was not taken into
account; they have to do with further imaginings concerning the
world. In the Gnostic text *Thunder Perfect Intellect*, Sophia says:

I am knowledge and ignorance
I am shame and boldness.
I am shameless; I am ashamed.
I am strength and I am fear.
I am war and peace.
Give heed to me.
I am the one who is disregarded and the great one.[1]

Every step we make through the world hand in hand with another casts shadows which we then walk into unaware, giving connections their color. The new form of relating asks us to stay with the colorful—not the light in the absence of the dark, not the dark in the absence of the light, and not shifting from one to the other. Being with another person in the world is enlivening and irritating. If it seems to be sometimes one and sometimes the other, the shifting back and forth means that we have lost the connection with the world and have fallen back into a "you and me," two egos who cannot find their I because the world is neglected. When we think we know where we are with our partner, then we are ignorant; and when we don't know where we are, that is the opening to knowing through the world. When we feel strength in our relationship, that is the opening to our fears, and our fears are needed to find the courage to find our strength.

When couples complain that they no longer have anything in common, such a complaint is usually heard as saying the pair no longer know each other, that they have lost the ability to communicate or to express their feelings. The complaint is also heard as saying that the two people no longer live in the same world. Here, however, the world has most likely been usurped by the egos of the individuals. World is taken to be "my world," as if the little sector with which I am involved has become my possession. In such circumstances, finding again what two people have in common, if it works at all, is no more than joint egotism. The therapy in this

direction has as its aim the convergence of two senses of "my world"
into a single sense of "our world." But what about Her world? How
do we, you and I, find the way there? Sophia, here under the name
of Isis, speaks concerning Her world:

> *I gave and ordained laws for men, which no one*
> *is able to change.*
> *I am she that is called goddess by women . . .*
> *I divided the earth from the heaven.*
> *I showed the path of the stars.*
> *I ordered the course of the sun and the moon.*
> *I devised business in the sea.*
> *I made strong the right.*
> *I brought together women and men.*
> *I appointed to women to bring their infants to birth*
> *in the tenth month.*
> *I ordained that parents should be loved by children.*
> *I laid punishment upon those disposed without natural*
> *affection toward their parents.*
> *I made with my brother Osiris an end to the eating of men.*
> *I revealed mysteries unto men.*
> *I taught men to honor images of the gods . . .*
> *I made the right to be stronger than gold and silver.*
> *I ordained that the true should be thought good.*
> *I am the Queen of rivers and winds and sea.*
> *No one is held in honor without my knowing it.*
> *I am the Queen of war.*
> *I am the Queen of the thunderbolt.*
> *I stir up the sea and I calm it.*
> *I am in the rays of the sun.*
> *I set free those in bonds.*
> *I overcome Fate.*[2]

The final declaration here is most important with respect to finding the way out of bondage to the ego and into the world with another. When there is only you and me, there can be no freedom. Relationship, when it involves just two people, is condemned to the laws of Fate; we are together in order to work out, work through, work on our karma, to work out our debts from the past. Love here is paying off one's debts. That relationships have this crucial dimension is in itself quite a revelation, and I do not want to suggest that avoiding such work is beneficial; I suspect, in fact, that we have such large debts to pay that often the breaking of a relationship is rebellion against this work. But, at the same time, the world offers the possibility of a true dimension of freedom; and without this dimension, it is likely that rebellion would be a necessity. If we work only on our fate, we are realizing only half of what we are; we are attending only to what we have been and not to what we can be.

The way to the dimension of freedom, indicates this passage, is in joining ourselves with the order of the world. First, this order, this arrangement of the world, is to be honored; it is the order of the goddess. She says, "I brought together women and men." That is to say, we are brought together through the world as soul. This bringing together of two into partnership is an aspect of the order of the world; it belongs to the arrangement of the heavens above and the Earth below; it belongs to the way in which the stars constellate and the planets, Sun, and Moon follow their complicated courses; with the mysterious depths of the oceans and the rhythms of the human body. The domains of family life, of just relations between people, of what is true and what is right, all belong to this order, Her order. We find the element of freedom within this ordering because here we are what we are intended to be by Her—not what we think we ought to be, as if the world were not involved.

If the arrangement of the cosmos is seen as a vast mechanism, then it seems as if freedom can be experienced only by finding how not to be a part of this mechanism, and learning how to turn this mechanism toward our own purposes. Such freedom is an illusion. Freedom cannot mean to stand outside of the universe, because there is no outside.

Our freedom is more to be located in the act of individualizing the universe through imagination, which requires full engagement. Such an imagination begins as Sophia does throughout this passage—she is engaged in self-praise. Entrance into the conscious recognition of our freedom within the universe begins with the capacity to praise. Sophia's self-praises, through which she tells us who she is and what she does, tell as much in the way they are presented as in the content. The form is one of singing, chanting, reciting, which saves the content from literalism by folding it into the act of imagination. The imagination here is one of everything in the universe as a song of praise.

The laws and the order and the arrangement of the world Sophia speaks are musical, the world as symphony. If one note in a musical composition is played off key, the whole composition is off. If a musician decides to go his or her own way in the middle of a symphony in order to express freedom, the free play of the whole is destroyed. On the other hand, musicians find true freedom when their individuality harmonizes with the whole. Freedom in relationship, it seems to me, concerns developing this capacity of heightening the expression of the whole.

Relating through the world can take us toward the capacity of a conscious, imagining I, because our I belongs to the world. In the Gnostic text *The Gospel of Eve*, Sophia says:

> *It is I who am you; and it is you who are me.*
> *And wherever you are, I am there.*
> *And I am sown in all; and you collect me from wherever*
>   *you wish.*
> *And while you collect me, it is your own self that you collect.*[3]

This passage makes us once again remember that the human body is not an object in the world, but world as individuated consciousness. Wherever we are, the whole world is also there, and everything in the world awaits its consciousness. That world consciousness is what can be called the self, or the I.

Why not, though, see all this as involving individual and world, instead of seeing the world as the third through which two individuals relate? In the triad of woman—world—man, woman is the gateway to wisdom; without woman, knowledge about the world would be possible, but not knowledge that is the world in the form of imagination. Knowledge that is only about the world has turned into a formula for destruction; this has been the way of man, through whom we have learned to place ourselves over and against the world. Relationship is a necessity, not for the sake of two individuals, but for the sake of the world; but, especially for the present and for the future, the direction of relationship has to be in the direction of the womanly. Ego knowledge of the world characterizes the past. Self-knowledge that is the world characterizes the future.

When is the future? The future, on one hand, is imagination, and thus the time of the future is whenever we experience the world in a fully conscious way. On the other hand, it is quite justifiable to ask whether such imaginal truth has any significance if it cannot be shared, if others do not imagine in the same way. But we can fall back into the ego and into the past if we go looking for a unified world and define unified as single. The whole point of relationships as important in the world and for the world is that there are as many worlds as there are relations. The primary question then becomes not what is the one and real world, but how can I relate my true experience to another whose world is different but also true?

Relationships between individuals may constitute the training and the discipline needed for such a new way of working in the world. Unless, however, the world herself is the third, attempts to relate what one experiences as true are bound to result in the attempt to have one view dominate over another. The presence of the world in the relationship makes it possible for one to say to another, "Oh, yes, I understand, it can also be seen in another way that is equally true."

The Future of Marriage

Marriage, as it presently exists, does not have the strong element of womanly characteristics I have been attempting to portray as ways of relating from the time current that comes to us from the future. Marriage is either a social contract that seeks to assure stability within society, or a religious vow sacralizing such a union. Marriage does have a meaning beyond the two people involved; the third in this instance is usually the social context on one hand and the family on the other. But marriage is more and more becoming a matter of individual interests, and individual desires now seem stronger than the social, religious, or family context implicated in it.

The difficulty that arises still is the expectation that the fact of marriage itself, of being married, has some sort of magical power that holds two individuals together. Marriage has been taken over into the economic realm, where social stability has become identified with financial debt. Rather than going into the world, this form of relating often takes the form of attempting to purchase the world and bring it home. And it turns out in such instances that two people do not stay together for each other or for the world, but perhaps for the family, for a time, and often for economic reasons.

Can there be more to this form of relationship? To approach this question, I must relinquish the legal, social, and even religious context of marriage as it presently exists and try to consider the significance of two individuals who come together through the medium of the world. Is such a triad temporary, needing after a time the forming of another triad, and perhaps yet another? Such a question would seem to assume that the world as the medium of connection lacks depth; and indeed if it is thought that sequences of relationships are implied by bringing marriage into question, then there has been misunderstanding of the true meaning of the world as soul. To be in service to soul, to Sophia, does not and cannot come about in a short time.

I recall reading about an unusual marriage indicating something of this new form of relating. What was unusual about the announcement is that the two people indicated in their wedding vows that serving the preservation of the rain forests was part of their vows to each other. This is admittedly an unusual instance, but it is very moving, and an indication of an awakening of a consciousness from the future. The question for the couple now is how to create a love that continuously includes the rain forests. How will these two people go about learning more about the world that is bringing them into connection? It is not hard to imagine that they are involved in a relationship of depth because the depth here comes from the side of the world. This couple has something to work for besides themselves. There are certainly many instances of couples working together, but mostly these mutual efforts are still oriented toward getting rather than giving. When mutual effort is directed toward giving, it is most likely that the relationship will be long-term if it can be focused on learning from the world rather on than bringing a system of improvement to the world.

How can this new form of marriage be sustained? How can working together in the world—in which intimate relationships are public rather than private—involve learning to perceive the world and each other as coming-to-be, value the Shadow as giving color and dimension and depth to relating, find freedom in belonging to the harmonious order of the world, and focus on developing the capacity to praise all things actually work? How can such qualities be taken into a lasting form of relating? No social forms exist today that support, nourish, and affirm approaching relationships in such ways.

Relating through the world can easily become lost in objectifying the world, so that working together in the world loses the aspect of also coming closer to each other. Work then takes over, and the relationship is forgotten. In such instances, the will to do something takes over, and the soul dimension is forgotten. On the other hand, the relationship can predominate, and the focus becomes on the temperament and inclinations of the individuals, in which case there is soul with no will. To complete our picture of relating from the future, we need an imagination of how this form of commitment is also making a new social form.

In 1119 A.D., nine knights, under the leadership of Hugo de Payens, began a social form of the future, known as the Knights Templar. During the course of a relatively few years, remarkable accomplishments of a soul and spirit nature were brought into the world—including the building of several hundred cathedrals, hospitals, a banking system, road systems. The Knights Templar were driven out of existence through the greed of Philip the Fair of France, who had fifty-four knights of this group brutally tortured and executed to gain access to the wealth of gold held by this group.

The Templars can be a significant image for the kind of world imagination we have been developing, because they operated out of the time current from the future. They foresaw the possibility of work in the world that was for the sake of the world. I am not suggesting that the Knights Templar be revived, but rather that we look at what made possible the development of a new social form that is akin to the one I have been attempting to describe.

The central question for the Knights Templar was how to hold together inner development with outer work in the world. Two maxims guided them. The first is *Non nobis, Domine, non nobis sed tuo nomini da gloriam:* "Not for us, Lord, not for us, but in honor of thy name." Can we now take up this maxim with Sophia at the center? "Not for us, Sophia, not for us, but in honor of thy name." To maintain the balance between growing in relationship and keeping the world as the third in the relationship, Sophia must be kept at the center, and in consciousness.

The second Templar maxim is: *Ora et Labora:* "Pray and Work." *Ora* refers to the work of inner development. In the present world, those who seek inner development usually separate this work from the outer work of daily life. As mentioned earlier, when inner development is separated from the world, it is always in danger of turning into spiritual or soul greed; soul development is easily taken to be for the good of oneself, not for the good of the world. *Labora* refers to outer work in the world. When work is separated from inner development, the result is what we see in the present time: Work ties itself more and more to economic life and becomes trapped in materialism. Can we also take up this maxim with Sophia at its center? Instead of *Ora et Labora* only, we could instead say, *Ora, Convive, et Labora:* "Pray, live together, and work." The addition of living together provides a midpoint between the inner-directed life of prayer, meditation, and soul development and the outer-directed working life—provided that living together as a couple consciously recognizes the third, the Soul of the World, as the medium of the connection.

In addition to honoring Sophia and dedicating our relationship to work in the world, another practical element is involved in this new marriage from the future. This element concerns what transpires between the couple, the communication that keeps the marriage open. Rather than a focus, as in the traditional form of relating, on expression of personal feelings to keep in connection with how we are getting along, an open conversation is needed here. Not, what do I feel and what do you feel, and what do we feel about each other, but how does what we are making together feel—is it whole, comprehensive; does it belong to the world, or is it being imposed on the world; are we still working out of imagination, or have we begun to lose this focus? These and a thousand questions like them can form a new mode of intimate conversation.

Does this mean that we are not concerned about the well-being of our partner, with how he or she is doing? No, this too is involved; but it is interwoven within the situation of an imagination of the world. Thus, this kind of conversation is intimate and close, at one and the same time close to each other and to the world.

IO

COMMUNITY AND FRIENDSHIP

WIDENING the sense of relationships suggests that we consider relationships beyond those of an intimate nature. This extended spectrum involves connections with others in which love does not seem to be involved. Typically, this realm of relationships with others in the world comes under the heading of community. I shall not use the word *community* much in what follows because it is too fraught with preconceptions. Community is one of those potent words that tend to obscure particularity because it has become overlaid with generalizations, idealizations, and abstractions.

The primary difficulty here is the belief that a community is supposed to be able to accomplish something that cannot be done by individuals alone. We hear so much today about how much people can do if they band together as a community—they can solve neighborhood violence, get rid of unwanted elements, work together for their own improvement, take matters into their own hands when the system ignores the real needs of people, become recognized as a force that cannot be ignored. And if community is not such a force, it at least gathers together people who can find commonality and understand each other when the larger world does not understand them: support groups of every sort.

Here we have a key insight, namely, that community, as usually understood, defines itself by being against other aspects of the world and gains power by gathering together numbers of conforming individuals. No matter how inclusive such a group may be, it defines itself in relation to what does not belong. The world sense of relationships that I want to explore concerns neither banding together nor needing anything to oppose in order to have definition and act in the world.

Individuality and Community

Individuality, as I have tried to show, is always in the process of coming to be. The closer we can get to this sense of individuality, the more possible it becomes to also experience the world as always in the process of coming to be. To be able to stay in this creative realm in which we and the world are activity, whatever content is gained as a result of experience must be constantly relinquished as a tool to be used. Otherwise we are relying on what we already know, and are not usually conscious that we are confronting the ever-new. The challenge of encountering the world through individuality is to meet the world through what we are coming to be, not through what we already know. This challenge is particularly acute in the domain of relationships.

When people meet and seem to sense a mutual interest, the possibility of deception is very great. With the development toward individuality, meeting another person directly is not possible, even though we think we do. I meet someone and this person seems to think exactly the way I do. This sort of meeting seems to be a rare occurrence and is bound to make people feel that they are together. I do not immediately sense that the other person does not really think the way I do, but rather mirrors back to me what I already think, and that I am doing the same in relation to what the other person thinks. We do not really think alike, but the similarities are usually detected at first, and not the differences. When the differences do emerge, they often cancel out the similarities.

Deception here is not deliberate and is not manipulative,

though it can easily become manipulative. One can quickly learn that the best way to get along with others is to mirror back to them what they already think. Organizations and corporate businesses tend to elicit from their members or employees only what management wants to hear, and members and employees quickly find out that the best way to be considered part of the group is to mirror back to those in charge what they already think. Such mutual deception is often called community building. The dynamic of mutual mirroring between people belongs to the processes of the ego, not the I. While many relationships have begun to change from ones that are clearly oriented toward power, based on strategies of winners and losers, to ones based on what are now called "win-win" strategies, the very terminology betrays the centrality of the ego.

In meeting another, being open to individuality while avoiding self-centered egotism may seem impossible, given the way I have described meeting, because the emphasis was placed on mutuality in the realm of thinking. One might well say that of course difficulties arise here because the emphasis is on trying to relate from the head rather than the heart. If we concern ourselves, not with whether another person thinks like I do, but with whether I like or dislike someone, is that not a better way to start relating? Liking or disliking, however, are forms of judgment in the emotional sphere. To be led by emotion is just as false as to be led by mutuality of thought.

Relating through emotion completely subjectivizes our connections with others. If an attraction exists in the form of good feeling, the source of the feeling remains obscure; similarly, if the feeling is one of antipathy, the source of this feeling also remains obscure. In both instances, however, we are not meeting the individuality of the other person, but only encountering confirmations of our own feelings. If I like or dislike someone, I feel as if I am detecting something about that person, when in fact I am only expressing something about myself. The difficulties of egotism are not circumvented by trying to take the route of feeling. Whether in the realm of thought or in the realm of feeling, people do not really meet other people, but are brought together more or less through mutual egotism.

We come now to a further exploration of the sense of the I, actually an elaboration on what has been pointed to thus far. I fear, however, that the true nature of the I, because it cannot be grasped exactly by concepts, continues to slip away the moment we get close to understanding it. So, let us start again, this time with the aim of revisioning connections with others in the world.

If we could imagine the moment, the very second before the I comes into expression, what is there? What is present from the viewpoint of the change from ego to I? Nothing. Nothing is present. The outer world of things, of nature, of animals, plants, and humans, is not present. Those many moments in which we come to the end of our rope and nothing any longer makes any sense, for example, are actually moments of coming close to the I. We usually cannot bear the feeling of approaching such a void and begin to feel as if we are going crazy. In such times, however, nothing is there but the empty shell of a world for us, and this empty shell is no more than the vestiges of the way the ego used to encounter the world and be filled with itself by taking and using what was given to it.

I am not reverting here to existentialism and the attempt to value angst. From the viewpoint of the ego, the world is always there; we may feel one way about it at one time and another way at another time, but the world goes on. However, someone who has approached the void cannot possibly come away from this experience without having a direct and immediate sense of the world in an entirely new way.

We may describe this new, emerging vision of the world as one in which the significance of each part of the world is equal to whole. One may look at a flower, and sense in the flower an invisible but nonetheless absolutely tangible quality of this single flower as being the whole of the world. The appearance of the world in this way is due to the awakening of the I. This description of the I supplements the descriptions previously given, and orients us to some new qualities of relationship.

We can perhaps begin to see some of the difficulties with the word *community*. This word usually results in the part being annihilated for the benefit of the whole; but the whole in such instances is an abstraction, an ideology, a sentiment, in which individual egos become submerged in a group ego, which can feel very satisfying. The even-momentary experience of a part of the world being perceived as the whole; however, sets us on a wholly different course. This little moment in which, with the sense of the part, the whole is given at the same time, is a true experience of the Soul of the World. At that moment the possibility exists of a complete change in the quality of relationships with others. One can thus experience another person as utterly particular, individual and unique while at the same time sensing that the whole world encompasses the individual. With such an attitude of approaching others, to imagine diminishing the part for the sake of the whole becomes inconceivable. Diminishing the part would only destroy the ability to sense the whole.

The Grail and World Relationships

The story of *Parzival* also gives us a picture of what I have just tried to describe When Gamuret, Parzival's father, married Belekane, a son named Feirefis was also born of that marriage. We hear nothing of him until the final stages of the book. The important scene is a battlefield fight between Parzival and Feirefis. The two do not know that they are brothers, for Feirefis is not a known knight. He is a stranger. Feirefis gets the best of the battle, and

Parzival's sword is broken. He seems doomed, but Feirefis will not fight an unarmed man. Instead, they sit down and talk, and in speaking with each other they discover that they are brothers.

In order to understand this scene, it is necessary to take Parzival here as an image of the I. Remember, he began his quest as the fool, and through his travels and mistakes and courage he becomes the holy fool. His encounters with the Sophia in her various aspects depict the development of the I. Feirefis is best understood as a figure picturing what was spoken of earlier as the nobility of the ego that develops strength by taking in all that the world has to offer. This nobility is pictured in the story through the fact that Feirefis wears armor bedecked with every precious jewel imaginable. He has taken earthly experience and crafted it into gemlike qualities, which we can imagine to be qualities like perseverance, truthfulness, and steadfastness.

Given this way of looking at Parzival and Feirefis, the remarkable aspect of this scene is that it is Feirefis, the stronger one in terms of getting along in the competitive sphere, who turns to Parzival to talk with him. That is, the I cannot come into expression in our lives on its own. We have to turn toward the I and do so out of the strength we have developed. This fact is most important because it is the basis for a healthy psychology. Depth psychology, because it has developed out of working with people who have come to the point of a breakdown of the ego, sometimes fosters the notion that the ego must go away before the soul finally gets attention. What is not given attention in depth psychology is that when this kind of situation occurs, it is only through the relatively healthy ego of the therapist that the patient begins to be able to face soul. The ego of the therapist, in effect, stands in for the less healthy ego of the patient.

Since this crucial role is not recognized, depth psychology promotes the demise of the ego as the entry into soul. What remains unseen is that this can only result in distortions of soul and of soul work. It can only result in an egotism of soul work because the ego, if it is not strong in its own right, will only take from the soul for its own purposes. On the other hand, ego psychologies, which foster the development of a strong ego, do so in the absence of tending to the soul factor and in complete ignorance of the I, and thus only strengthen the personality, fostering adjustment rather than transformation.

In this part of *Parzival,* what happens next is of significance for the question at hand, the question of relationships with others in the world. Both Parzival and Feirefis become members of King Arthur's Round Table. The Round Table represents worldly power. But, the nature of the Round Table changes with the entrance of these two members; it is now to be pictured as the Grail working into the world. A ceremony takes place in which Feirefis gives gifts to everyone; the ego has changed through coming into relation with the I. When we are confined to the ego sense of the world, we live as if scarcity rules the world, and thus we have to try to get whatever we need for ourselves, even if it seems to mean depriving someone else. With the awakened sense of the I comes the capacity to approach the world out of the sense of abundance, the sense that everyone is able to have exactly what is needed.

The Grail is nothing other than the Soul of the World in unity with the individual soul, now fully conscious and lived as the sense of the I. One more crucial event in the story must take place, however, to make the Grail fully available to everyone; that is, one more capacity must be developed in order to begin to live full and individual imaginative consciousness in unity with the Soul of the World. Parzival must go back into the Grail Castle.

The Grail King, Amfortas, had received a wound in the genitals that would not heal as a result of pursuing romantic love of a woman. In terms of what we have said about love, Amfortas, rather than developing a sense of love from out of the future, became caught in an older form of love. He sought love for his own self-interests. Parzival now can heal Amfortas, something that he had failed to do earlier, when he had come to the Grail Castle and had seen the wonders of the Grail and the suffering king, but had failed to ask the Grail question. Now, through his own development, he is able to ask this question.

He approaches the wounded, suffering Amfortas, and with everything in his being he asks, "How can I help?" This is not an intellectual question, or even a question out of genuine sentiment; it is a moment of seeing the whole world as being one with the individual. It is a moment of giving everything one is and can be for the benefit of another, without losing oneself in the process.

This picture of what the Grail is about helps us to look quite differently at going about relationships with others. Instead of wondering whether we have anything in common with the person we meet, whether we think similarly about things, or whether we like the person or not, we can begin to try to imagine approaching another person differently. The question, How can I help? must not, however, be taken literally. Literalizing here would result in our imposing helping onto others. A whole industry has sprung up due to such literalization. And, instead of actually helping, literalizing the question of help turns out to mean that that the helping professions profess to have exactly what they think others need. If we have an awakened imaginative sense that is at the same time awake to the world as well as the individual, then the question is actually something like, How can I care for your soul as an individual manifestation of the Soul of the World?

Naturally, such a question cannot be asked literally because it would not be understood. Such a question is rather a state of being expressing a whole host of living questions: How can I help without in the process diminishing your freedom? How can I help in a way that does not try to fix you as if you were a broken mechanism? How can I simply be with you where you are? How can I help without being a professional helper? How can I help without abstracting you from the context of your being a vital and inextricable part of the whole of the world? How can I help without seeking some tangible or intangible reward for myself? Because the questions are not literal, they cannot be answered; they are questions to be lived with and lived within as a different and new way of relating with others in the world.

Let us pursue this new way of relating with others in the world even further, for helping is subject to many illusions. Ordinarily, when I imagine being of help to someone, even in the enlarged sense which is portrayed above, the desire to help is followed by a sequence of actions. In order to be of help, I do something which progresses as if from step to step. Maybe, at first, I concentrate on simply trying to understand another person, simply listening. Then, I set out and perhaps try to mirror back to the person my understanding. And, if I am careful, I do not then propose a plan to the other person, but step by step, let him or her work out a course of action.

Living out of the sense of the Grail question does not proceed in such a manner. The Grail question is not one that simply initiates relationship. Since it is a question one lives within, it means that each moment is lived as a question. Conclusions have to be released at the moment they come into form. I have to use my intellect to understand what is needed by the other person. But, then, I have to recognize that there is a side to intellect that is not content to just be present, but wants to form what is understood into a form of literal action. How can we find the way through such a dilemma?

This little dilemma is really one filled with world significance. The whole of *Parzival,* in fact, can be seen as a working through this dilemma. Feirefis, born of Belekane, enters the story as a figure from the East. He may be seen as representing an Eastern aspect to the way we ask questions, the aspect of not needing to do anything but take in and listen in an attitude of nobility and unselfishness. When this aspect of quest-ioning consciousness is developed, it becomes meditation. Developed on its own, this dimension of questioning finally takes a certain form of relating to others, the form of compassion.

One dimension of what makes Feirefis such an interesting figure is that where we find him at the end of the story is in the West. His presence there in the West is seen as strange, magnificent, beautiful, noble. The moment in his fight with Parzival when he has won the battle and could kill him, but instead stops, can be seen as a moment of noble compassion. Compassion does produce results in the world, but they are always miraculous results. Healing can occur through no more than a look from the eyes of one filled with compassion.

In contrast, the Round Table is a picture of the West, where the focus is on achievement. The moment a question is initiated, a plan of action is required, and it has to be one that is assured of results. Action is what counts, and a question without an answer is not of much interest. A question without pursuit of an answer is unheard of. The image of the Round Table shows us that a question is often looked at, not just as a single individual might see it, but from all angles. There were twelve places at the Round Table, and thus we can imagine viewing a question from twelve perspectives. But Arthur is the head of the Round Table, and the direction of action is through that aspect of the questioning part of ourselves that takes authority and initiates doing something.

This part of the questioning seems to lack a meditative dimension. Results then are visualized as taking place on the same plane as the presenting question. If someone seems, for example, to be suffering from anxiety, which can be felt in the body, something is looked for, like a tranquilizer, to eliminate the problem. When we listen only with the aim of initiating action, the soul element does not enter, so there can be no transformation to a different level. The soul element requires time, rumination, fantasy, without being pressed to action.

Parzival brings together the capacity for living in questions, characteristic of the East, and the necessity for action, characteristic of the West, into a middle way between the inner act of meditation and the outer act of action. The middle path is one in which the unending process of the questioning is what is important; this means that the value of the Grail quest is in the questing itself, a balance between meditative consciousness and action. This middle way is the way of love. Here, then, we can begin to get yet another feeling for the quality of love that comes not from the past, but from the future. Love is not just a deep inner feeling, love as meditation, nor is it action and deed in the world, love as demonstration. Love, in this new sense, is deep interior contemplation so strong and so intense that it constantly moves out into the world, but does so in ways that are always unexpected.

The way of love is another way of describing the binding between the individual soul and the Soul of the World. Previously, I described Sophia as the Holy Trinosophia. Holding questions in an inner way that leads to meditative consciousness refers to the Sophia at the center of the Earth, for here it is a matter of waiting as Sophia waits. Doing something in a way that does not seek a preplanned, singularly oriented result, but realizes that entering deeply into soul is already a doing, refers to the Sophia that is the activity of the creating elements of the world. This form of world activity is one in which every element is related to every other element.

Love as it has been developed here refers to the Sophia who is returned to the pleroma, the fullness of the all, the Sophia who encircles both world and individual. The I expresses the Holy Trinosophia in a completely individual way. This I brings about the union of the three aspects of the Trinosophia.

International Relationships

The coming together of Feirefis and Parzival, of compassion and love, of East and West, shows that the way of Sophia is international. This internationalism can be taken at many different levels. First, we should note that actual appearances, visions, of Sophia have taken place in India, Mexico, the United States, Russia, Egypt, Eastern Europe—just about everywhere on Earth. Although she is often spoken of as "the Lady," her appearances cannot all be said to be in the form of Mary, and they have not been confined to people connected with a particular religion, region, nationality, or culture.

In contrast to the internationalism of Sophia, the world is now strongly oriented either toward nationalism or toward multiculturalism. Nationalism is a collective form of egotism, and multiculturalism tends to be the attempt to lump many forms of egotism into the same space. Nationalism is built on the old forms of love through the blood, a reversion to clan and tribe that negates the possibility of evolving into individuality. Multiculturalism amounts to different groups showing their nationalism to others and demanding respect, but it does not seek to destroy the identities of other cultures. Multiculturalism is built on self-love and the maintaining of group identity by building up self-feeling.

Vladimir Soloviev, a Russian philosopher who lived from 1853 to 1900, devoted his life to bringing about a Sophianic world. He himself had three different visions of the Sophia. The first took place in Moscow, when he was nine years old. The second took place in London, and the third in Egypt. To experience a true vision is unusual, to say the least. To experience a vision on three different continents may be saying something about the nature of the one who appears, as well as about the one who sees. We might feel that, after all, a heavenly being can appear anywhere. But, it is not quite accurate to say that Sophia is a heavenly being. As we have described her, she exists in three aspects, as heavenly being, earthly being, and soul being. What seems to be significant here is that in all aspects she is international. Because she brings all things of the Earth into unity without the loss of particularity, this unifying quality of Sophia also applies to international relations.

This last part of this final chapter will not turn into a treatise on international relations. The appearances of Sophia throughout the world have one characteristic that ought to be taken as instruction—those who see her are the children, the troubled, the lost, the wounded, the hurt, the exiled. And when we look at who is most injured by what goes on in conflicts between countries, there can be no doubt that it is first and foremost the children; then the women; then the aged.

When countries cannot seem to find ways to relate, they either impose economic sanctions or wage war, and then hinder relief efforts oriented toward humanitarian aid. Waging war in the present world is something entirely new because the element of soul is being attacked, murdered, and plundered. Children, women, and the aged most exemplify the free expression of soul in the world, so we should not be tricked into believing that the reasons present wars are carried out have to do primarily with disputes over land, race, oil, or economics. These motives are at the surface only. Deeper and more subconscious, the motivation is to prevent soul and thereby stop the evolution toward individuality.

What is it that wants to prevent this evolution? Why would attempts to revert to the past sense of collective blood soul, through nationalism, or to seek self-feeling through multiculturalism be preferred to development toward individuality from the future? Depth psychology would most likely say that this is due to great fear that the past may be lost altogether, and that if people could only see that the collective past always lives in the life of the soul there would be no need to literalize the past. I see the difficulty not as a fear of losing the past, but as a fear of encountering the future.

The future concerns having to create love rather than being nourished by what already exists, or hoping to be nourished by the forces of love from the past. The task of having to create love opens an abyss. We have to do it without knowing how, and even without being supported by reliance on archetypal images, which would also take us toward the past, even if in an imaginal way.

The prospect of creative love is frightening. Nonetheless, one would think there would be eagerness for the experiment. What needs to be recognized, however, is that when the abyss is opened up another factor enters, the polarity of creative love—evil. I have hovered around the question of evil throughout this writing, and wanted to avoid introducing it directly as a topic. Nonetheless, it is necessary to talk about it. We must, however, avoid on the one hand absolute definitions, fundamentalist in tone; on the other hand we must avoid taking the stance that evil is not in the world, but only within each of us as our Shadow. The approach to evil taken here is only in relation to individuality and the World Soul.

The old polarities of love versus hate, good versus evil, do not serve well in times of complexity where most things are mixed. Once we extend the sense of love beyond that of an emotion, a personal feeling, its polarity is no longer hate. Hate simply becomes one of the instruments of evil. Thus, the notion of good as the polarity of evil also needs to be put aside. Evil is complex, and in our time is often disguised as the good. The atomic bomb was not seen as an evil, just as an effective weapon of war. I also do not want to speak of love as something absolutely good. When a type of love that belongs to the past, where it was a good, is lived outside of its proper element of time, it can become an evil—though only if not relinquished at the proper time. Such love even may be an important basis for further kinds of love.

One helpful way of looking at the question of evil, developed extensively by Rudolf Steiner, is based on the notion of imbalance. Here, an absolutizing of evil is avoided. First, we recognize that two values that seem opposed to each other both tend in the direction of evil when they are both out of balance with something else. For example, the polarity of cowardice might seem to be recklessness, but both of these are an imbalance of the quality of bravery. The opposite of apathy might be sensitivity, but here again, the balance is found in between, concern.

A further aspect of this way of approaching evil is that the transformation of evil seen as imbalance requires not rejection or avoidance, but developing the capacity to enter into either side of the polarity and transform it from within. Cowardice is not solved by trying to avoid it, because one would most likely be drawn into recklessness. But if one is able to face cowardice, bravery becomes possible; similarly, if one is able to face recklessness, bravery also becomes possible.

Another most important aspect of looking at evil as imbalance is that the two directions of imbalance are quite different. One direction of imbalance tends toward inner emotional life, cowardice and sensitivity in the examples above; the other direction of imbalance, in my examples, tends toward an excessively impersonal outwardness, recklessness and apathy. The place of balance can thus be seen as equivalent to the place of union of the individual soul with the Soul of the World, what has been described as the I.

Another insight made possible through this way of approaching evil is that the way through imbalance has to do with bringing a certain kind of objectivity to the personal and bringing the intimacy of the personal to those things which seem most impersonal. This way of looking at things shows clearly that the personal cannot be equated with soul, as it often tends to be. There is actually no more soul in being excessively personal than in being a cold-hearted technocrat. Sentimentality, emotional effusiveness, always speaking directly from feelings is probably imbalance. On the other side, cold technology and science are not the enemy of soul. If these ways of working in the world were eliminated, we would not have soul, but a mixture of New Age nonsense masquerading as physics and a variety of reversions to things from the past that look exotic and seem to be more healthy, but in reality hold back evolution. If we were able to approach our own individual soul life with the discipline and rigor characteristic of science, radical changes in science and technology would soon result; they would be transformed through soul.

Friendship and the World Soul

Due to difficulties in coming to a place of balance, the international, world-unifying destiny of Sophia is greatly hindered by nationalism and slowed by multiculturalism. In addition, the complexities of evil make maintaining the balance of the middle element of soul difficult to keep clear. If advancement goes too quickly and too technically, as in the former Soviet Union, then the backward movement of nationalism threatens to return.

The question that emerges from this set of dynamics is how the I can be strengthened as the conscious nexus of connection between individual soul and World Soul. If this connection is tenuous, the I will lose its creative capacity and fall back into forms of egotism. The binding of the individual soul with the World Soul concerns perhaps the highest and deepest form of love, that of friendship. This form of love more than any other strengthens the connection between individual soul and World Soul.

Vladimir Soloviev spoke of Sophia as "Eternal Friend." The love that is friendship, *philia,* is perhaps more intimate than any other kind of love. Another Russian scholar of Sophia, Pavel Florensky, developed an understanding of this mode of love, saying that friendship is that reality making the soul's inner unity fully possible.[1] While the I was previously spoken of as creative love, we can now go on to characterize this creative love as being similar to friendship. One who is awake to the sense of the world as soul experiences the whole cosmic, natural, and human world as an intimate friend, through whom one finds the perfect reflection of one's individual soul. The ancient maxim that the human being is a microcosm reflecting the whole macrocosm finds its modern expression in the notion of friendship. Friendship is the knowledge of oneself through the eyes of another, one who truly sees you because Sophia sees through the eyes of love. In other words, Sophia, the Soul of the World, radiates love for the individual, which brings the individual soul out of the darkness of the subconscious so that it can live in the light as the I. We find ourselves in the face of the world. The world is thus truly a thou, an Eternal Friend.

Friendship implies an equal exchange. This means that the world too finds her identity, finds herself, in connection with the individual I. Through our friendship with her, she becomes conscious of herself. She is drawn out of the darkness of Chaos and lives as the world that we now see as living. Soloviev's poem "On Lake Saima in Winter" beautifully expresses this coming of the world into light:[2]

> *Here in this deep silence,*
> *My inner eye, my waking heart beholds*
> *Your image fair, still unchanged,*
> *O Queen, ruler of the pines and rocks!*
>
> *Pure as the snow upon far*
>   *mountain summits,*
> *Wise as the thought-filled silence*
>   *of this winter night,*
>
> *Radiant as the glorious Aurora*
>   *of the North,*
> *I behold you now, dark Chaos's*
>   *happy, smiling child!*

Seeing the world as friend is like seeing the world for the first time. Such a seeing is actually a metaphysical sharing of one's being with the beloved other, as the other shares her being with us. The world is the cause and motivation for our own self-knowledge, and in each of us, every single individual, she also comes to self-knowledge. As pictured by Soloviev, she becomes air, pines, rocks, mountains, aurora, which existed perhaps only as brooding presences before being known by a friend. Through the intimacy of friendship, all of the things of the world become radiant, shining, alive, and the Earth as a whole becomes the Earth-Sun.

The individual soul and the World Soul thus do not exist as one over against the other, but as interpenetrating realities. This world situation, we must admit, still exists mainly as potentiality. Some few have had actual experiences, such as Soloviev, who gives us a glimpse of a possible future that is coming to meet us. The international friendship of Sophia indicates that this future is being offered simultaneously in all places and to all people and will not occur as a wave starting somewhere and proceeding step by step. In this way, She has assured that she will not be captured by a single religion, taken up as someone's promotional project, or become a spiritual movement of the masses.

What is it about true, abiding friendship that is so strengthening for the relation between individual soul and World Soul? Florensky takes us further into the imagination of friendship by indicating that its strength is due to a surprising element, jealousy. Usually, we imagine jealousy to be a destructive element in love, one that, when it rears its ugly head, threatens to dissolve relationships. But, if we look more closely at the actual operation of jealousy, we have to admit that it is always present in relationships, no matter how secure they might feel. Rather than trying to get rid of it, should we not try to discern how it apparently belongs to the very nature of relating? And, if friendship is the most creative form of love, we shall find that jealousy is its guardian.

The creative power of love would remain something general and abstract if there were not something present within this power itself that intensifies, focuses, and particularizes love. The friendship that characterizes the binding between individual soul and World Soul is not an abstraction that is being used to try to describe an impersonal world process. When this friendship is actually lived, it is an ongoing exchange between lover and beloved. Thus, when we see the world being treated in any way other than as beloved, it is as if she is being taken from us. The resulting pain is no better described than as the pangs of jealousy.

And, when we turn away from her to pursue our little desires as if they were more important than she, she falls into darkness and brooding, an expression of her jealousy. At such times, the world seems to be uninviting, turned in toward herself, a world of things and objects rather than the radiance of Soul. The presence of jealousy in all other forms of love can be seen as refractions of the jealously guarded love between individual soul and World Soul. Jealousy is the faithful shadow of love.

Because of jealousy, love can never become a habit; jealousy is always in the background as the indicator that love is a continuous work. This faithful servant turns us back to the work at hand whenever we become forgetful and unconscious. Jealousy does not in its primal quality have to do with possessing the beloved. What we usually call jealousy, what I feel when one whom I believe to be mine and mine alone turns instead toward another, is an emotion based in desire and reveals the connection as one of greed. Behind such emotional jealousy is the fact that the one loved is actually being treated as an object. But souls can never be possessed the way that objects are possessed. The reciprocal relation between individual soul and World Soul, their intimate union as the conscious I, expresses interdependence, not codependence. Jealousy here is nothing other than the zeal of love, the intensity of its vitality.

In this extended sense of jealousy as a quality of soul relationship rather than possessiveness of an object of desire, we are called
to see jealousy as the patron, guardian, and faithful attendant that
transforms soul itself into love. Through the jealously guarded
friendship between individual soul and World Soul, soul is in the
process of transformation into love. The Wisdom of the world concerns this gradual transformation, which is the destiny of the Earth.
It is, in fact, what is meant by saying that the Earth is the planet
of love. Earth is not simply the place and location where love
occurs. All of the forms of love have to do with more than what
goes on between human beings alone; they are preparations that
help us develop the capacities needed for our part in world destiny.

Love is not the fate of Earth. The fate of Earth is the same as
that of any living being—to be born, develop, age, and die. Destiny concerns the transformations that can take place that alter fate.
And, in this time, in which the fate of Earth is being accelerated
at a high rate, we perhaps have little time to see deeply into her
soul, which is also our soul, and to take up the course of destiny.

NOTES

CHAPTER 1

1. Sigmund Freud, *The Future of an Illusion* (New York: W.W. Norton & Co., 1961), pp. 15-16.
2. Sigmund Freud, *Civilization and Its Discontents* (New York: W.W. Norton & Co., 1961), p. 26.
3. Sigmund Freud, *Beyond the Pleasure Principle* (New York: W.W. Norton & Co., 1961), p. 21.
4. Sigmund Freud, *The Interpretation of Dreams,* trans. James Strachey (New York: Avon Books, 1965), pp. 575-76.
5. Marc I. Barasch, *The Healing Path: A Soul Approach to Illness* (San Francisco: J.P. Tarcher/G.P. Putnam, 1993).
6. Rudolf Steiner, "Death and Immortality in the Light of Spiritual Science," unpublished lecture delivered in Bremen, Germany, December 12, 1911.
7. Trevor Ravenscroft and T. Wallace-Murphy, *The Mark of the Beast* (New York: Citadel Press, 1992).

CHAPTER 2

1. Walter Johannes Stein, *The Death of Merlin: Arthurian Myth and Alchemy* (Edinburgh: Floris Books, 1989), pp. 19-20.
2. For a complete view of the concept of the I as it has evolved in the history of philosophy, see Rudolf Steiner, *Individualism in Philosophy* (Spring Valley, NY: Anthroposophic Press, 1989).

CHAPTER 3

1. Caitlin Matthews, *Sophia, Goddess of Wisdom: The Divine Feminine from Black Goddess to World Soul* (London: Mandala/HarperCollins, 1991).

2. Vladimir Soloviev, *Lectures on Godmanhood* (London: Dennis Dobson Ltd., 1948), p. 178.

3. G.R.S. Mead, *Pistis Sophia* (Secaucus, NJ: University Books Inc., 1974).

4. Printed in Robert Powell, *The Most Holy Trinosophia* (Great Barrington, MA: Golden Stone Press, 1989).

CHAPTER 4

1. Steiner, like Jung, has the problem of being taken up in entirely literal ways by hosts of followers, in spite of his own imaginative mode of thinking. He has the additional problem of requiring a demanding, dedicated study that is as transformative of ego life as Jung's demanding and dedicated study is transformative of psychic life. What follows is not a study of Steiner, however, but does draw on what he saw, connecting it with modern depth psychology, and bringing this into relation with the Soul of the World.

2. Rudolf Steiner, *The Wisdom of Man, of the Soul, and of the Spirit* (Spring Valley, NY: Anthroposophic Press, 1971).

3. Vladimir Soloviev, *The Meaning of Love*, trans. Thomas R. Beyer, Jr. (Hudson, NY: Lindisfarne Press, 1985).

4. Text provided by the Embassy of the Czech and Slovak Federal Republic, 3900 Linnean Avenue (Spring of Freedom Lane) N.W., Washington, D.C. 20008.

5. *Ibid.*

CHAPTER 5

1. Ernst Lehrs, *Man or Matter* (London: Rudolf Steiner Press, 1985), p. 308.

2. Wilhelm Reich, *Ether, God and Devil/Cosmic Superimposition* (New York: The Noonday Press, 1973), pp. 116-17.

CHAPTER 6

1. For a further elaboration on the relation between dreaming and the etheric body, see Rudolf Steiner, *The Evolution of Consciousness as Revealed through Initiation-Knowledge*, trans. V.E. Watkin and C. Davy (London: Rudolf Steiner Press, 1991).

CHAPTER 7

1. William Irwin Thompson, *The American Replacement of Nature* (New York: Doubleday/Currency, 1991).
2. For an exploration of the senses based on Rudolf Steiner see A. Soesman, *The Twelve Senses,* trans. Jacob Cornelis (Glos, U.K.: Hawthorn Press, n.d.).

CHAPTER 8

1. Rudolf Steiner, *Spiritual Science and Medicine* (London: Rudolf Steiner Press, 1975), p. 88.
2. *Ibid.,* p. 119.
3. Arthur Guirdham, *Obsession: Psychic Forces and Evil in the Causation of Disease* (London: C.W. Daniel Co., 1972), p. 8.

CHAPTER 9

1. J. M. Robinson, ed. *The Nag Hammadi Library* (Leiden: E.J. Brill, 1977), pp. 272-73.
2. Quoted in F.C. Grant, *Hellenistic Religions* (Indianapolis: Bobbs-Merrill, 1953), pp. 132-33.
3. B. Layton, trans. *The Gnostic Scriptures* (London: SCM Press Ltd., 1987), p. 205.

CHAPTER 10

1. For an exposition of the concept of jealousy in the work of Florensky, see Robert Slesinski, *Pavel Florensky: A Metaphysics of Love* (Crestwood, NY: St. Vladimir's Seminary Press, 1984).
2. From Paul M. Allen, *Vladimir Soloviev: Russian Mystic* (Blauvelt, NY: Steinerbooks, 1978), p. 449.